dtv

dtv
_____
portrait

Series editor Martin Sulzer-Reichel

Martha Schad was born in 1939. After studying history and art history at the University of Augsburg, she took her doctorate with a thesis on "Die Frauen des Hauses Fugger von der Lilie" (*The Women of the House of Fugger von der Lilie*). Ms. Schad is known for her writings on female historical figures (the queens of Bavaria; Empress Elisabeth and her daughters; Women against Hitler; Hitler's Spy Princess and Stalin's Daughter – The Life of Swetlana Allilujewa), and has published the exchange of letters between Cosima Wagner and Ludwig II of Bavaria. Her biography *Elisabeth von Österreich* has already appeared in the dtv portrait series.

Ludwig II

by Martha Schad

Deutscher Taschenbuch Verlag

For Dorothea, Peter, Barbara and Brigitte
June 17, 2000

Deutscher Taschenbuch Verlag
Friedrichstr. 1a
80801 Munich
Germany
December 2001
4. edition Dezember 2006
First published 2000
© 2000 of the German edition and © 2001 of the English edition:
Deutscher Taschenbuch Verlag GmbH & Co. KG, München

Cover design by Balk & Brumshagen
Translated by Sally Schreiber, Isny, Germany
English editing and typesetting by APE Intl., Richmond, Va.
Cover photography: Picture by Ferdinand Piloty (AKG, Berlin)
Layout by Agents – Producers – Editors, Overath, Germany
Printed in Germany by APPL, Wemding, Germany
ISBN-13: 978-3-423-08520-7
ISBN-10: 3-423-08520-5

Contents

1 King Ludwig II in the robe of a Grand Master of the Bavarian Order of the Knights of Saint George. Painting by Gabriel Schachtinger, completed one year after Ludwig's death, 1887.

Hereditary Prince, Crown Prince, King

"It is a magnificent feeling to be a father."

The long-wished-for child: hereditary prince Ludwig

Cannon shots thundered out into the silence of the night at the Castle of Nymphenburg on August 25, 1845. There, at the summer seat of the kings and princes of Bavaria, located at that time far from the gates of the capital and royal residence of Munich, the long-hoped-for son had been born to Crown Prince Maximilian of Bavaria and his wife Marie.

The hereditary prince entered the world in the castle's Green Salon. After more than eighteen hours of labor, Crown Princess Marie gazed at her "little angel" lying in the small bed next to hers and thanked God for the great blessing.

Only a day after his birth, the castle was festively decorated and glittered with lights as the eightyfour-year-old archbishop Baron Lothar Anselm von Gebsattel christened the infant Otto Friedrich Wilhelm Ludwig. Two kings stood as godparents to the child: his grand uncle, Frederick William IV of Prussia, and his uncle, Otto of Greece, who was unable to

> **Crown Prince Maximilian described the events surrounding the birth of his first son in a letter to his brother-in-law, Prince Adalbert of Prussia:**
> "These lines are to inform you of the joyful news that the Lord has blessed our precious Marie with a sweet, strong boy. He was born on my father's birthday, which made him very happy. As you may imagine, I certainly did not take this serious event, which now fortunately lies behind us, thank God, lightly. I arranged everything with utmost detail and great care; ... both my parents were living with us and wanted to be close; my mother attended Marie with tender love; you can imagine that I almost never left her bedside and that I, too, suffered much. Labor began around 4 o'clock in the morning—Marie asked for me after 6 o'clock—and it was half an hour after midnight when the little boy came into this world. Hearing his first cry was a magnificent moment. Marie immediately forgot her pain. She had suffered long and much, but bore it all admirably, even touchingly. She and the little one are—thanks be to God—well and are sleeping long and deep; it is a magnificent feeling to be a father!"

2   King Ludwig I of Bavaria.
Painting by Joseph Stieler, 1825.

be present. Because the baby's royal mother could not yet attend the ceremony, the little prince was entrusted to the queen's faithful lady-in-waiting, Euphrasia von Pillemont. The baby's grandfather, King Ludwig I of Bavaria, proudly carried his new grandson, clad in a lace-trimmed christening robe, in his arms. Prince Adalbert, Maximilian's youngest brother, carried the christening candle.

A few days after the baptism Ludwig I was able to persuade the young parents to call the child Ludwig, arguing that the day of his birth was not only the feast day of Saint Ludwig in the Catholic Church, but also happened to be the old king's own birthday. From this point on the boy, baptized Otto, was known as Ludwig.

In celebration of the prince's birth, a multitude of gifts arrived at the royal residence from near and far. Among them were short poems, such as the lines penned by a certain Greger that were particularly touching in their simplicity:

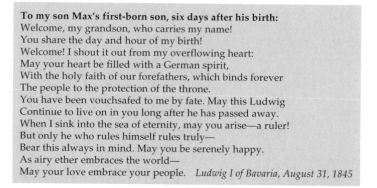

To my son Max's first-born son, six days after his birth:
Welcome, my grandson, who carries my name!
You share the day and hour of my birth!
Welcome! I shout it out from my overflowing heart:
May your heart be filled with a German spirit,
With the holy faith of our forefathers, which binds forever
The people to the protection of the throne.
You have been vouchsafed to me by fate. May this Ludwig
Continue to live on in you long after he has passed away.
When I sink into the sea of eternity, may you arise—a ruler!
But only he who rules himself rules truly—
Bear this always in mind. May you be serenely happy.
As airy ether embraces the world—
May your love embrace your people.   *Ludwig I of Bavaria, August 31, 1845*

Sleep little prince! Sleep
sweetly!
Paradise blossoms for you,
angels serve and bring
blessings to you!

Sleep little prince! Sleep
sweetly!
Paradise blossoms for you,
where eternal spring
reigns and brings you
abundant joy.

3   King Otto I of Greece, ca. 1833.

Ludwig's mother, Queen Marie, a niece of King Frederick William IV of Prussia, had become crown princess of Bavaria in October 1842. Born on October 15, 1825, in Berlin as the youngest of seven children, she resided in her early years with her parents in the Rhineland cities of Cologne and Mainz. In addition, the family had a summer residence at Fischbach in Silesia, far to the east in what is today a part of Poland. After making a futile circuit of the courts of Europe in search of a suitable bride, the thirty-year-old Crown Prince Maximilian had proposed marriage to the sixteen-year-old Hohenzollern Princess Marie in December 1841, but the formal engagement, scheduled for January 1842 in Berlin, had to be postponed because the bride fell ill with measles. Furthermore, before the wedding could take place, another ceremony had precedence in the royal Prussian house: the bride had to be confirmed. In contrast to the traditionally Catholic Wittelsbach family of Bavaria, the Hohenzollerns were Protest-

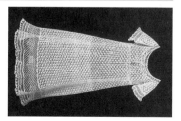

4   Ludwig's christening robe,
25 inches (63 cm) long, was
exquisite. The extremely delicate,
finely knitted sleeves of the robe
were appliquéd with linen
Valenciennes lace; the lower
seam was of cotton filet.

5 Interior view of All Saints Church, Munich, site of the Catholic wedding ceremony of Crown Prince Maximilian of Bavaria and Marie of Prussia.

ant. To Marie's great joy, her Catholic fiancé attended her confirmation ceremony, which was celebrated in the Protestant village church at Fischbach. On October 5, 1842, a proxy Protestant marriage ceremony took place in Berlin. Standing in for the bridegroom, who could not attend, was Prince William of Prussia, the future Emperor William I of Germany. It seems an ironic turn of fate that the man who years later would withdraw sovereignty from Ludwig II knelt next to his mother at the altar in 1842.

The journey of the crown princess from Berlin to Munich resembled a triumphal procession, and her arrival in the residence in Munich was equally stirring. Against all court eti-

Crown Princess Marie very much wished her parents to be present during the birth of her first child. However, they never saw their Bavarian grandson. Marie's mother, Princess Marianne von Hessen-Homburg (1785–1846), was the daughter of Landgrave Friedrich V of Hesse-Homburg and Caroline von Hessen-Darmstadt. Her father, Wilhelm (1781–1851), belonged to the Hohenzollern dynasty which had also produced King Frederick the Great of Prussia (Frederick II). Marie's parents were en route to Bavaria to meet their grandchild when Princess Marianne suddenly became ill in Darmstadt. They had

Grandduchess Mathilde von Hessen-Darmstadt, sister of the groom, described the wedding ceremony:
"Max and little Marie are the picture of happiness, thank God. As she walked from the altar on Max's arm, we thought she looked like a guardian angel. As we stepped over the threshold of the church, it was very moving when a sudden beam of sunlight broke from the clouded heavens and cast a friendly light on the earth. Max cried a great deal during the ceremony; Marie was fully under control, but very pale—her expression cleared up as she left the altar."

quette, the young woman leapt from the carriage, ran to her fiancé and embraced him. The Catholic wedding ceremony took place in the royal chapel of All Saints on October 12, Saint Maximilian's day. By February 1843, Marie was pregnant with her first child, but miscarried after the third month.

After the successful birth of the infant Ludwig, a strong and healthy farm wife from Miesbach was employed as a wet nurse. The baby developed beautifully during the first eight months, but then the wet nurse became ill of a "vehement fever that had infected the brain"—obviously meningitis—and died. That this early loss deeply affected the little boy was immediately apparent: the abrupt weaning caused his health to deteriorate so severely that he almost died. Suffering from fever cramps, he remained sickly for months. The loss of his wet nurse might also explain Ludwig's later inclina-

to return to Berlin where—in April—she passed away attended by Crown Prince Maximilian and her daughters, Marie and Elisabeth.

6   Marie of Prussia. Painting by Joseph Stieler, 1843.

tion to seek out "mother-like, or more precisely foster-mother-like, relationships with those whom he supported." After the death of his wet nurse, Sybille Meilhaus was appointed as governess to the little hereditary prince.

The choice proved to be a sound one: the child began to recover, gained weight, and soon had his first three teeth. Court child-rearing practices of the time normally implied that children were left in the care of a governess while the parents went about fulfilling their court duties without hindrance. Marie, however, took care of her son personally, insofar as her numerous social obligations allowed. In July 1846, as the crown princess was returning from a trip to Hohenschwangau, the governess Sybille Meilhaus travelled with the little prince from Munich to meet her. Shortly before they arrived at the castle, however, the horses shied and the carriage with the governess and child almost overturned. Fortunately, nobody was hurt in the incident and, on August 25, 1846, the entire family was able to celebrate Ludwig's first birthday.

On Ludwig's second birthday, in August 1847, his parents were spending time in the small, fashionable resort of Schlangenbad in the Taunus Mountains in central Germany. Marie therefore composed a birthday letter "to her dear little child" in Munich wishing him God's blessings. She also bought him many toys, among them Austrian soldiers and some

7   Ludwig's governess Sybille Meilhaus was born on August 20, 1814, in Hanau as the daughter of the wine seller Johann Meilhaus and his wife Magdalena Thekla. At the age of 45, she married calvary general August Ludwig, Baron von Leonrod, and died more than twenty years later on April 20, 1881.

Ludwig, with whom she corresponded until her death, commemorated her with a neo-gothic monument of Carrara marble in the Catholic cemetery at Augsburg.

marbles. "Miss Meilhaus will give you more toys today. Last night I dreamt of you and I will think of you the whole day long, my dear little child! Papa sends you many kisses and wishes you happiness and blessings." That Crown Prince Maximilian gave his wife flowers and a brooch in the form of a little angel on their son's birthday would certainly seem to indicate that the parents did, indeed, enjoy an affectionate relationship.

A close and very loving relationship soon developed between Ludwig and his governess, whom he affectionately called "Aja" or "Millau". To this warm-hearted and motherly mentor, who was at once well-educated and pious, the eight-year-old crown prince dedicated the following verses on Christmas 1853:

Dear Meilhaus,

If I could do more than
    wish, if I could give,
Best Millau, as tender as
    you are pure,
Then every one of your
    days would pass
As happily as the beauti-
    ful celebration today.
But, since I have nothing
    better to give,
Accept my gift of gratitude.
My heart is filled with love
    and respect for you,
Dear one, keep loving me
    in the future!

8   Ludwig, at age two, with a picture book. Watercolor by E. Rietschel, 1847.

Revolutionary unrest and birth of a second son, Otto

"Otto is as lovely as it is possible to be."

On March 20, 1848, King Ludwig I abdicated, handing the crown on to his son Maximilian. As rumors of an imminent revolution began to spread, with the threat of possible riots in Munich, Duchess Ludovika and Duke Maximilian of Bavaria offered Marie, who was in the last months of her third preg-

The Abdication of King Ludwig I

Ludwig I, since 1825 King of Bavaria, was a very liberal-minded man with a distinctive inclination for culture and the sciences. In the beginning, he enthusiastically supported the European liberation movements as well as the liberal constitution of 1818, and transformed the capital city, Munich, into a metropolis. However, even in the 1830s his political decisions became increasingly conservative. Considering himself a ruler by God's grace, he rejected the political "interference" of the people, and therefore came under growing political pressure from the democratic movements that developed before the German Revolution of 1848. Under these circumstances, his affair with Lola Montez proved disastrous. The dancer Maria Dolores Gilbert (1818–1861), daughter of a Scottish officer and a Creole mother, had arrived in Munich in 1846. She not only won the affection of her audience but also the king's heart. Her breathtaking career and immense influence on Ludwig's policy decisions earned her the nickname "Bavarian Mme. Pompadour." Until today, her stage name Lola Montez remains synonymous for women in show business who build their careers on intimate relationships with politicians or nobles and try exert political influence through sexual favors. The liaison between the king and the dancer came very opportunely for the opposition

party in Bavaria. They claimed that the influence of the foreigner was taking the king away from his political duties. When Ludwig made his mistress the Countess of Landsfeld against the opposition of the nobility and simultaneously rejected the reproaches of the clergy (he supposedly replied to the archbishop of Munich, "You stay with your *stola* (stole), I stay with my Lola"), he also lost the support of the conservatives. Riots in Munich forced him to abdicate the throne in March 1848.

9 Lola Montez. Contemporary caricature.

nancy, shelter with them in Possenhofen. Marie decided to remain in the royal residence, however, and on April 27, 1848, gave birth to a second son, two months early.

Although the scandalous events surrounding the abdication of Ludwig I had severely damaged the image of the royal house, the populace responded sympathetically to the birth of another son, scion of the ancient houses of both Hohenzollern and Wittelsbach—that is, of Prussia and Bavaria. On April 29, the child was baptized Otto Luitpold Wilhelm Adalbert Waldemar in the king's quarters of the royal residence. Once again, King Otto of Greece became godfather, but at this christening, the candle-bearers were the infant's two-and-a-half-year-old brother Ludwig as well as his three-year-old cousin Ludwig, the later Ludwig III.

Meanwhile, Queen Marie was following "the political events in Berlin" in the newspapers. Well informed about activities in Prussia, she took it as a sign of God's grace that in Bavaria, in spite of all the revolutionary ideas circling about, no serious attempts to abolish kingship or restrict the royal power occurred, as was happening in the rest of Germany— "truly a rare gift of God in these sad times, where all bonds between the king and his subjects seem to be breaking apart." In fact, it was thanks to Marie that the bond between the king and his people was strengthened. Her youth and warmth had won the hearts of the people, and she was actually much more popular than her husband, who appeared introverted, preferred High German to the Bavarian dialect and was generally regarded as "serious, reticent, withdrawn and passionless." In his memoirs, Paul Heyse noted that the people approached the queen more comfortably than they did "His Majesty".

After all the revolutionary confusions, life at the royal court returned to normalcy in the second half of 1848. The

> To be king during times like these is a difficult task, a demanding burden, which the Lord has placed on my poor king; but he carries it with faith and childlike trust in HIM. HE will help him.
>
> *Marie of Bavaria, 1848*

10 Queen Marie with her young sons Ludwig and Otto in 1848. Lithograph.

royal couple moved into the suite in the residence previously inhabited by Ludwig I. When not in residence in Munich, the family lived in Hohenschwangau Castle, and in 1849, they established a second summer residence at the foot of the Fürstenstein near Berchtesgaden. To please his wife, the newly crowned king also had a cottage built at Blöckenau resembling his mother-in-law's Swiss chalet, the so-called Mariannen Cottage in Fischbach. He also began construction of a beautiful summer house on Rose Island in Lake Starnberg.

In Munich, official duties left the king little time for his sons. He saw them only at noon during the second breakfast and in the evening during the court dinner. On these occasions, he did no more than greet the children. Youthful pranks or unfulfilled duties, on the other hand, he punished by beating, a measure that he considered indispensable to transforming the boys into effective princes. Ludwig confessed later, "We trembled before our father." The princes felt that their father treated them condescendingly. Thus, father and sons lived at a distance, and it saddened Ludwig that his father noticed him only in passing with a few cold and arrogant words. The king, in turn, complained that Ludwig was not willing to share any of his interests. Nor did it help the father-

Maximilian II Joseph
Born on November 28, 1811, in Munich, he ascended to the Bavarian throne after the abdication of his father, Ludwig I, in March 1848. Central to Maximilian's foreign policy were questions concerning the future shaping of Germany and the power balance between Austria and Prussia, in which Bavaria was forced to take sides. A great patron of the arts and sciences, he founded the Historical Commission of the Academy in 1858 and reigned until his untimely death on March 10, 1864.

son relationship that Maximilian, who was plagued with severe headaches, spent months in Italy or with his brother Otto in Greece in the hope that the warmer climate would heal him. Queen Marie also often complained that Maximilian left her alone for long periods.

Whatever deprivation of paternal warmth the two princes may have experienced, they did not grow up isolated from other children. From many surviving letters, we know that the children of the various branches of the House of Wittelsbach visited and corresponded with each other frequently. For many years the sons of Luitpold of Bavaria, Leopold and Ludwig (later King Ludwig III), spent time with their royal cousins, Ludwig and Otto, every Sunday.

In the winter months, the palace resounded with the children's "wild games"—which expanded into the Nymphenburg gardens during the summer. Contrary to all court etiquette, the young queen chased through the residence playing hide-and-seek with her children while the boys beamed with joy. Among their playmates were also a commoner—the son of the surgeon Gietl—and Helene von Dönniges, daughter of the historian and statesman Wilhelm von Dönniges, who had the greatest influence on the king at the court. Helene von Dönniges described the time when she was the "chosen playmate of the crown prince

11   Maximilian II Joseph, King of Bavaria, in the robe of a Grand Master of the Order of the Knights of Hubertus. Painting by Wilhelm von Kaulbach, 1852/1853.

as a very happy one." Although the children had an abundance of playthings, their youthful games were largely imaginative and fantastic. "Our highest ideal was to pretend that we were elves. Curtains were transformed into flowers and winged garments in which we shrouded ourselves and in which we lived—in our youthful imaginations, we enjoyed the most enchanting experiences." Helene also recalled the "spitting game"—a favorite of almost all children—or twisting the heads of the big, handsome, sculpted tin soldiers. Looking at a picture book could end in "bitter fighting"—the crown prince being the victor with some of "my red-golden hair torn in his small hands."

Prince Leopold, Ludwig's cousin, noted in his memoirs that their grandmother Therese, the wife of Ludwig I, gathered all the children at the Wittelsbach palace every Sunday between noon and 1:00 P.M. and let them paint lithographs with watercolors. The little princes and princesses used to work with great intensity because their grandmother bought their art works for a few coins, thus enhancing their modest allowances. This tradition ended abruptly in 1854, however, when Therese succumbed to the cholera epidemic then raging in Munich. Family celebrations at their grandparents' house were great fun. Ludwig I and Helene von Dönniges always served hot chocolate, huge pretzels and chocolate from Altenburg with potato cakes. The children were very impressed that their grandfather served them personally. Adding to the fascination of the visits were the two parrots and a pair of monkeys, brought back from Greece by Maximilian, that their grandmother kept in the tower.

The boys' mother, Queen Marie, loved the Bavarian Alps, and in fact the Hohenzollern princess from the flatlands surrounding Berlin became Bavaria's first woman mountain

The Bavarian royal couple made the effort to communicate with their sons frequently. When they were separated from the children for a longer time they often wrote letters to them. In return, the princes' replies often contained pressed flowers for their parents. When their father was staying in Rome in March 1857, the almost nine-year-old Otto wrote, "I would so much like to pick flowers with you in Rome! Here, I do not find anything but little violets. I am studying with Mr. Klass every day; I already write little essays and do quite difficult arithmetic. Most of all I love history and geography. ... My dear father,

climber. Ludwig and Otto enjoyed accompanying their mother on her mountain excursions. Together they climbed the Säuling, taking three-and-a-half hours to get from Hohenschwangau to the summit. The twelve-year-old Ludwig expressed his excitement about these climbs in detailed letters to his grandfather. In the area around Berchtesgaden, the princes and their mother hiked to the Obersee, the Ice Chapel and to Wimbach. In addition, they also hiked to the Schartzkehl and the Koenigsalpe—but the crown prince complained "bitterly" to his grandfather that he was not allowed to accompany his mother to the Untersberg, which she climbed in 1858.

One day, Marie took her sons with her to search for edelweiss growing in the rocky cliffs of the mountain lake Obersee accompanied by two ladies-in-waiting, Count de la Rosée, Baron Wulffen, and two mountain guides. This expedition on September 10, 1859, took a dramatic turn. On the way to Fischunkel on the Obersee, the queen sent the two "mountain princes" ahead to pick edelweiss. With them was Baron Wulffen, who suffered such a bad fall on the mountain ledge that he could no longer get up. The queen, who was fleeter of foot than anyone else in the party, hurried back to Obersee to get a doctor while Ludwig ran for a priest. The injured baron recovered—but fell again when he returned to the same place a year later.

The year 1854 inaugurated great changes for the crown prince. On May 1, Major General Baron Theodor Basselet de la Rosée—known as *la rosée du soir de la Bavière*, the "Bavarian sunset"—succeeded the beloved governess Sybille Meilhaus as princely educator. He was aided in his task by Baron Emil von Wulffen and Major Carl von Orff, grandfather of the composer Carl Orff. Ludwig also received theological instruction from the dean of the cathedral, Georg Carl von Reindl,

I look forward to seeing you very much and to spending time in the country.—I respectfully kiss your hand and am, with all my love, your grateful son."

and the abbot of St. Bonifaz, Daniel Haneberg, who also became the prince's confessor.

As soon as their schooling began, at the personal command of their father, the princes received 90 pennies pocket money per month—a sum which was increased over the years. Ludwig used his first allowance to buy his mother a locket.

During the school year, the princes were no longer allowed to travel, but their father made an exception in 1855 when the town fathers of Nuremberg requested that their "royal lord and his honoured wife" permit the princes make an appearance during a five-week visit of the royal family to the proud city. When ten-year-old Ludwig and seven-year-old Otto finally arrived by train in Nuremberg, they ran into their mother's arms, kissed her hands and snuggled in her embraces. The reception hall of the castle in Nuremberg—a city long famed for its toy production—was so filled with toys that the excited boys did not know what to play with first.

In 1856, Ludwig began preparation for the university, devoting eight hours a day to the study of the humanities with the philologist Franz Steininger, a professor at the Maximilian Hischool in Munich. Ludwig's program included Latin, Greek, German and history. Otto proved to be a more apt pupil than his older brother; nonetheless, Ludwig registered at the University of Munich at the age of 17. There he attended lectures and took part in several seminars, studying physics with Johann Jolly, chemistry with Justus von Liebig, and logic and the history of philosophy with Franz Steininger.

On August 29, 1863, the crown prince attained his majority, in a year that proved to be of particular significance to the Bavarian royal family in view of the coming wars of German

Dear grandfather!
I would like to thank you from the bottom of my heart for your tender letter and good wishes, as well as for the wonderful poem, which I enjoyed very much. On my birthday the weather was wonderful. I got up at 4:30 A.M. and went fishing. I caught a splendid nine-and-a-half-pound sturgeon. Later, I received many good wishes and presents: a picture from All Saints Church, illustrations of the Nibelungen epic by Schnorr, a pin with a swan, a book on Faust and on the works of Shakespeare and

12   Nymphenburg Castle and park in Munich.

unification in 1866 and 1870/1871. In September 1863, the German princes gathered in Frankfurt under the patronage of Emperor Francis Joseph of Austria to discuss the reform of the German Federation. In the unification question, Austria and Prussia vied for ascendancy, and at King Maximilian's request Queen Marie asked her uncle, King William I of Prussia—Francis Joseph's rival—to attend the princely diet in Frankfurt. The Prussian king, slighting the Austrian initiative, ignored her request and proceeded instead to Bad Gastein. When the monarch interrupted his journey in Munich, accompanied by Count Otto von Bismarck, however, Maximilian asked his wife to "keep a firm hold" on the Prussian king until he and the other princes could hurry back to Munich and take him along to Frankfurt. Bismarck, whose

others. ... A delegation from Munich arrived and we invited them to stay for the festive meal. In the afternoon, we drove to the Swiss Chalet and at night, there was an illumination. Mother thanks you very much for your letter and kisses your hand; Otto does, too. ... I am looking forward to seeing you, dear grandfather, in good health very soon! Kissing your hand, I remain, with tender love, your grateful grandson Ludwig.

To Ludwig I, describing his 18th birthday

intention was to unify the German empire under Prussian leadership and to exclude Austria, managed to foil the possibility that William would attend the diet in Frankfurt, thereby dealing a lethal blow to Austria's final attempt to establish a unified German state under Austrian leadership. At the same time, Austria was unable to achieve a unification of the empire without Prussia, because the so-called German middle states opposed the concept of a German nation.

Ludwig, however, pursued his education relatively untouched by these important political events. After attending the lectures in Munich, he intended to register at Göttingen University, but the sudden death of his father intervened. During the night of March 10, 1864, the two princes and their mother knelt at Maximilian's bedside, but were finally prevailed upon to retire to bed. At 5:00 A.M. their father called for them to bid farewell to his wife and his sons. Only four weeks after Maximilian's death Ludwig's educator, Baron Basselet de la Rosée, also passed away, leaving the young king to reign without the support of his experienced adviser.

The Ruler

"… I bring a heart to the throne. …"

Although severely shaken by his father's death, the crown prince was proclaimed king the very same day. In accepting the crown, Ludwig assumed a heavy inheritance. Both at home and abroad, he faced numerous political challenges. In his coronation oath on March 11, 1864, he swore, "God Almighty has taken my precious and beloved father away from this earth. I am unable to express the feelings coursing through my breast. It is both a great and a heavy task that lies before me. I trust in God to send me the light and power to master it. I shall reign true to the oath I have sworn just now and in the spirit of our constitution that has proven itself trustworthy for half a century. My beloved Bavaria's well-being and Germany's greatness are my declared goals. I ask you all to support me in these difficult duties."

During their father's lifetime, the princes Ludwig and Otto had not often been seen publicly in Munich. When they attended the funeral procession all eyes were resting on them, and Ludwig made a deep impression. The young king was athletic and physically very well developed, a good rider and an avid swimmer. "He had a pleasant voice and his diction was excellent," commented Count Lerchenfeld, Bavaria's representative in Berlin, "but he was too ceremonious and absolutely without humor."

At the beginning of his reign, the young king attended to affairs of state with utmost diligence. Those secretaries who had assumed he would be satisfied with the role of a marionette

God (I look to Him with firm trust) will surely not deny me his support in this difficult task. I bring a heart to the throne, which beats with fatherly love for the people and glows for its well-being—all Bavarians may trust that! I shall do whatever lies in my power to make my people happy. May their well-being and peace be the guide for my own salvation and peace!

Excerpt from the coronation speech of Ludwig II, on March 11, 1864

He was the most handsome young man I have ever seen. His tall, slender body was perfectly symmetrical. His rich, slightly curled hair and the slight touch of a moustache gave his head a resemblance to those magnificient antique works of art through which we gained our first impressions of what the ancient Greeks considered masculinity.

The writer Clara Tschudi on her impression of Ludwig II, 1864

were soon abused of their illusion. Their hopes of dominating the king were quickly shattered as he lost no time making changes in his cabinet.

After Ludwig's accession to the throne, the letters of his grandfather, Ludwig I, indicate that the older man now hoped to exert a greater political influence than he had in the past. He probably expected more openness in his grandson in this regard, but in fact, he found the opposite. Ludwig I therefore found it necessary to remind the young king of his family position in order to enforce his will: "Do not be taken in by flatterers, do not cast aside your grandfather's wealth of experience—he only wants your best. Do not allow history to say that Ludwig II dug the grave of the monarchy." Nonetheless, the letters also reveal a certain amount of sympathy: "Poor Ludwig! He who ascends the throne at eighteen gives up his youth; at that age he cannot yet have acquired the experience and ability to handle state affairs so needed in times like these!"

The Bavarian constitution of 1818, which had been amended in 1848, conceived of the king in his role of head of state as unifying all state power in his own hand. As his power stemmed not from the people but directly from God through an act of grace, the king's person was sacred.

Like his predecessors on the Bavarian throne, Ludwig controlled the general political policy of the land, was the ulti-

The secretaries arrive between 8:30 and 9:30 to 10:00 in the morning. Hofmann comes twice a week around 10:00 or 11:00 A.M., a state secretary comes every morning at 11:00 A.M., then I take my second breakfast and receive audiences at noon, then I drive and walk. At 4:00 P.M. is dinner, and at 6:00 P.M. I receive one of the secretaries, each in turn. Then Leinfelder reads me the newspaper, usually until 9:00 P.M., then I have tea.

To Sybille Meilhaus about his workday, 1864

mate court of appeal in legal issues, commanded the Bavarian army, and appointed and dismissed ministers. The connection between the royal government and the king was formed by the cabinet secretariat, with only the cabinet secretary having direct access to the monarch.

Until the very last days of his life, Ludwig carried out his supervisory duty over the administration. During his twenty-two-year reign, his signature appeared on 100,000 documents. Moreover, his attention was not limited to the mere formality of a signature. In many cases the files bear the king's remarks, testimony that he was well acquainted with the documents.

Ludwig appointed a total of six new presidents of the ministerial council and of the ministry of the royal house and the exterior. Although they all belonged to the liberal camp, their political goals were entirely different from each other. In contrast, Prussia enjoyed—with one interruption—a single minister-president and foreign minister between 1862 and 1890: namely Otto von Bismarck, who intervened intensively in Bavarian affairs after the founding of the German Empire. The Prussian ambassador, Baron Georg von Werthern, acted both officially and unofficially in accordance with Bismarck's intentions. For him, the political standpoint of the Bavarian

13   Ludwig II of Bavaria in the uniform of a general with coronation cape. Painting by Ferdinand Piloty, 1865.

populace, of whom "the large majority was still completely unreckonable" was "in the hands of a secret, powerful party whose roots lay outside the country"—that is, in the Curia of the Roman Catholic Church. The king he termed a cowardly, duplicitous clown.

The king's advisory board consisted of a thirty-member state council. The bicameral parliament was made up of an aristocratic upper house, or First Chamber of Deputies, and a lower house, the Second Chamber of Representatives. The latter, elected for six years, was known as the Landtag, or state parliament, after 1848. During Ludwig's reign, a two-party system was in play. The parliamentary majority lay in the hands of the conservative Catholic party, which was rooted in the countryside and patriotically oriented toward a whole-German concept. Ludwig, however, consistently appointed his ministers from the liberal camp. No law could be passed without ratification by the king and the upper house, and the king also had the authority to convene, extend, postpone, or dissolve the Landtag. The powers of both houses were limited to presenting petitions, complaints, and proposals.

Initially, Baron Ludwig von der Pfordten was chairman of the ministerial council, a post which he had also held under Maximilian II. Similarly, Franz Seraph von Pfistermeister had already

14   The kingdom of Bavaria with its eight counties, Nuremberg, 1836.

Yesterday I accepted Pfordten's letter of resignation. The wretched man who conducted himself badly on our behalf is gone. Pfi and Pfo are now without influence.

To Cosima von Bülow,
December 30, 1866

served in the court secretariat under Ludwig's father. After the peace treaty with Prussia in 1866 (cf. p. 71ff.) the king dismissed "Pfi" and "Pfo", that is, Pfistermeister and von der Pfordten, from the "most exalted personal service" for their machinations against the king's personal favorite, the composer Richard Wagner—a step which Wagner himself had often demanded. Lorenz von Düfflipp replaced Pfistermeister, and Johann von Lutz, a rather opportunistic liberal, became secretary to the king in 1866 to 1867. Subsequently Lutz replaced Justice Minister Eduard von Bomhard, remaining in office until 1871, and in 1869 he simultaneously assumed the offices of Interior Secretary and Secretary of Church and School Affairs. In 1880, Lutz became president of the ministerial council.

Supported by Richard Wagner, Chlodwig, Prince of Hohenlohe-Schillingsfürst, succeeded von der Pfordten in spite of the fact that the older King Ludwig I, who had been allowed to retain his title upon abdication, warned his grandson against Hohenlohe. The young king explained to Ludwig, however, that he had taken a dislike to von der Pforten because his policies had failed. The controversial prince was also supported by Max, Count of Holnstein. This thirty-one-year-old adjutant and later master of the stables was the stereotype of a rugged, traditional Bavarian horseman, and later gained considerable influence over the king. Indeed, the domestic policies of the newly appointed minister-president met with both Wagner's and the king's approval.

Encouraged by Hohenlohe, Ludwig set himself vehemently against the new doctrine of papal infallibility, which he saw as an infringement of his royal sovereignty. In this spirit, he approved of the draft distributed by the important Munich theologian Ignaz Döllinger of April 9, 1869, which

In 1864, the pope had published the encyclical *Quanta cura* in which he vehemently attacked the principles of liberalism, especially its development in Prussia. Together with the dogma of the infallibility of the pope, the encyclical was considered a provocation by many of the powerful Protestant circles who supported an economic liberalism. Especially in Prussia, under Bismarck's leadership, the position of the Catholic Church was considered a danger for the young national state, and the issue was divisive in other German states as well. Two political movements, the **Montanists** and the **Ultramontanists**—those who either appealed to the various European governments to join together to block the coming Vatican Council from making the threatening proposal a decree. This affair earned the king the enmity of the Ultramontanists, those who recognized the sovereignty of the Vatican on the other side of the Alps, that is, "on the far side of the mountains", in particular the Jesuits. The magnitude of the dispute even led to intrigues aimed at forcing Ludwig to abdicate. The king prevailed, however, and a year later it was the Jesuits who faced banishment from Bavaria. In spite of this success, Hohenlohe's opposition to papal infallibility resulted in a parliamentary vote of no confidence in both houses, resulting in his resignation. The king accepted the minister's resignation—albeit with reservations—on February 18, 1870, at which point the unaffiliated Count Otto Camillus Hugo von Bray-Steinburg, who had earlier served as Bavaria's ambassador in Vienna and Berlin, St. Petersburg and Paris, took over Hohenlohe's portfolio.

Within two years after the young king ascended the throne, it became clear that he did not enjoy life in Munich. He took every possible opportunity to flee into the Alps, whose foothills begin just south of the capital city. In 1865, for example, he spent only 68 of his official 296 days of official duty at the royal residence in the city. Nonetheless, Ludwig sought to carry out the business of government. His ministers often had great trouble locating him, especially in summer, when the king moved about from one hunting lodge to another as the spirit moved him. A cabinet member, for example, after numerous requests for an audience, might suddenly be summoned to some distant corner of the mountains from one hour to the next. Ludwig himself is reputed once to have remarked, "I wouldn't want to be my own cabinet secretary for anything in the world." Sometimes comical situations

rejected or supported the position of the Catholic Church "beyond the mountains" (the Alps) began to form. In Bavaria this conflict proved particularly difficult, since there the interconnections between the clergy and secular powers were very close. In Prussia, Bismarck used the conflict to eliminate the Catholic Center Party, which had been established in 1870, as "enemies of the Reich." The developing Kulturkampf (cultural conflict) became a serious battle. In 1871, Bismarck issued his famous "Clauses" and the "Law against the Jesuits," through which he gained control over and limited the influence of the clerics. He established

arose, as when a meadow in front of the forest lodge in Alt-lach on Lake Walchen had to serve as the "seat of government." There Ludwig sat in his travel clothes, Scottish Tam-o-Shanter perched on his head. Before him, dressed in a formal black coat and carrying his top hat under his arm, stood his head of Cabinet, informing him in stentorian tones of the incoming ministerial requests and proposals. The whole scene was punctuated from time to time by the sound of a cowbell. Next to the table stood the king's favorite horse, the gray mare Cosa Rara, and behind, the camp of the king's mounted servants.

Ludwig II and Technology

"Really to fly with you through the air. ..."

Ludwig took a great interest in the technical developments that marked the beginning of the industrial revolution in Bavaria in the second half of the 19th century. He incorporated iron and glass construction into his own building programs, introduced steam power, electricity and telephones, and was fascinated with the idea of flight.

Together with Friedrich Brandt, the court engineer, Ludwig forged plans for a flying machine to carry him over the Alpsee near Hohenschwangau. From the platform of the palace courtyard, a gondola built in the shape of a peacock was to operate on a simple rope pulley and transport the king across a distance of 4068 feet (1240 m) and lift him 162.7 feet (49.6 m) up to Sperbersau. Because the intended path passed directly over the Alpsee, no proper support was available, resulting in a slack rope. In answer to this problem, a plan was

civil marriage and placed the public school system under the supervision of the secular political power. The qualification of pastors was established through state exams and the "Bread Basket Law" of 1875 withdrew from the church all financial contributions by the state if the clergy did not bend to the secular power. Although other German states did not accept these measures to the same extent as Prussia, the conflict nevertheless led to a deep split between Catholic and Protestant citizens everywhere. Consultations with the Vatican were not resumed until 1878 when the confrontations were no longer endurable.

developed to suspend the gondola, still attached to the rope, from a balloon that would be sent into the air during the "journey." Although Ludwig put the twenty-three-year-old engineer under great pressure, the project could not be realized at that time. Ludwig wrote to Brandt, "Really to fly through the air with you ... that is my fondest wish, you and I, removed from the earth."

Later, at the end of his life, Ludwig's desire to fly would serve as evidence of mental illness and proof of the king's "excessive imagination, which completely disdains all limits of reality and possibility." Nonetheless, Ludwig's desire to fly was not unrealistic. A mere five years after the king's death, in 1891, Otto Lilienthal accomplished one of the first flights across several hundred yards.

15   Hohenschwangau Castle, one of Ludwig's favorite seats in the early years of his reign. It was from this castle that he planned to build a cable-car connection into the valley.

Court celebrations

The king's royal duties included attendance at court ceremonies, balls and the traditional New Year's reception in Munich. Ludwig withdrew himself from all such occasions as far as possible. Most important of the ceremonies at court requiring the king's presence was the Festival of the Knights of St. George, the most magnificent of all the public displays of the monarchy. Duke Albrecht IV had founded the order, then known as the "Brotherhood of St. George," in 1496 for courtiers, counts, knights and imperial knights. In the spring of 1729, Prince-Elector Karl Albrecht revived the order as a function belonging to the House of Wittelsbach, calling it the Bavarian Military Knightly Order of St. George. The reigning king was simultaneously the head and grand master of the order. In 1871 the Order received new statutes, which defined tasks to be carried out in a spirit of Christian charity, particularly the erection of hospitals in Nymphenburg and Brückenau.

The first ceremony to be held by the Order after Ludwig's ascension to the throne was scheduled for 1865, but the king cancelled it because he felt ill. The next took place on April 24, 1866—but without the presence of the king, who sent his uncle Luitpold as his proxy. The following year, Ludwig finally determined to participate in the festival, wearing the elaborate

16   Ludwig II in the costume of a Knight of St. George. Sixty-eight meters of silken satin went into the making of the royal blue cloak, which was decorated with extremely intricate embroidery. Marble statue by Friedrich Ochs, based on the model by the sculptor Elisabeth Ney, 1870.

regalia of the Order, but canceled once again in 1880: "His Majesty the King felt himself so unwell and irritated last night, that his Most Exalted Personage does not deem himself capable of sustaining the festivities of the Order." The notice was delivered so late, however, that the invited members of the Order could not be properly informed. Two days later, all the members had to appear once again in their Burgundian dress uniforms. The ceremonies with the king began in the inner audience chamber of the Imperial Room of the residence. Around 11:00 the knights were scheduled to come together in a plenary session, and shortly before 12:00 noon, a procession made its way through the residence to the ancient court church, which had been decorated with particular splendor for the festivities. The magnificent throne of the Grand Master stood on the pulpit side of the church, and the important priors of the Order took their places in front of the altar. During the three-hour-long high mass, the king dubbed the new knights with a ceremonial blow to the helmet and armor.

Another traditional ceremony took place on Holy Thursday before Easter, in which the feet of twelve worthy but impoverished old men were washed. After a mass celebrated in the royal Church of All Saints, the monarch, together with princes and noblemen from the three highest ranks at court, betook themselves to the chapel, where a light evening meal was served. They then proceeded to the Hall of Hercules, where the twelve men selected for the foot-washing ceremony were seated at the south entry wall of the chamber on a dark red platform erected for the occasion. The men were dressed in black and wore violet berets. Close to them stood family members and twelve girls, who, like the old men, had been clothed at court expense. The king then removed his hat and sable robe, the Master of Court handed him a vessel of water, while the subdeacon supported

17　Ludwig preferred to send a ▶ proxy to the ceremony of the washing of the feet on Holy Thursday. In 1884, as shown in this engraving, he was represented by Deacon Jakob von Türk.

a bowl under the men's feet. The king poured water over the naked feet of each man and dried them with a towel handed to him by the court marshal. Afterward the king hung a small blue-and-white bag filled with money around each man's neck. In conclusion, the recipients participated in a meal, at which wine was served. After a prayer of thanksgiving, the king returned to his chambers. Ludwig himself performed this devotion only rarely; instead, he designated high-ranking officials of the Catholic Church to carry it out for him.

Among the few family celebrations ordered by the king himself was a feast in honor of the newly married Archduchess Gisela, daughter of Empress Elisabeth of Austria, and Prince Leopold of Bavaria in the Court Ballroom of the Ceremonial Hall of the residence in Munich on April 30, 1873.

For the daughter of his greatly revered cousin, the Austrian empress, Ludwig even arranged a ceremonial entry into Munich, both the capital and royal seat of the realm. An honor guard of the king's personal regiment paraded in front of the train station as the newly married couple arrived from Vienna. Before them stood the ceremonial coach known as "The Great." This would be the only occasion on which the king's personal coach, built according to models from Versailles, was ever used. Pulled by six magnificent horses, the new Bavarian princess and her husband entered the city.

Ludwig further honored the daughter of the imperial house of Austria by receiving her at the foot of the stairs at the royal residence and leading her to the wing of the house built for the monarchs. There Queen Mother Marie and the entire royal family awaited her. It must be also accounted a great honor that the king, who by this time lived an extremely retired life, had ordered an official banquet for the couple. Ludwig sat on a raised platform in the midst of the royal family. In honor of the young princess, the Austrian national anthem sounded forth at her entry into the hall. The king rose from his seat and drank to the health of the newly-weds, succeeded by the wedding marches from *A Midsummer Night's Dream* and *Lohengrin*, as well as "Hail to Our King, Hail." The court ballet outdid itself with offerings, and court servants and chamber servants served the meal.

In the new winter garden that the king had built onto his opulent private chambers, a more intimate celebration was held for the couple. Princess Gisela was particularly pleased by the brightly lit garden and a raft trip around the small lake, rippling with artificially produced waves. Prince Leopold, who survived his cousin Ludwig by 44 years, later remembered these festivities as the only such occasion that he experienced at the Bavarian court.

This generous reception for the daughter of the Austrian empress might very well have led to political problems. The Prussian ambassador interpreted it as a "marked demonstration" of Bavarian sympathy toward Austria. His advisers requested Ludwig to stress to Berlin that he had no political intentions, but was only expressing his particular regard for Duchess Gisela.

18   Duchess Gisela of Austria, daughter of Empress Elisabeth, married back into Austria. Her husband was the Wittelsbach prince, Leopold of Bavaria.

The King's Journeys

Among the duties of every Bavarian king were regular journeys to various parts of the kingdom. Such contact was particularly important in Swabia and Franconia, which had been added to the traditional territory of Bavaria only in 1801 in the course of the Naponleonic wars. In these areas, the visits of the king and royal family were necessary in order to awaken and foster the inhabitants' sense of belonging to their new state. These visits of state followed a set formula.

Two years after ascending the throne, however, Ludwig had still not presented himself to his people. Eduard von Bomhard, minister of justice, pressed the recalcitrant king to take up his travel duties, whether to the military parade grounds of Franconia to the north or to the more distant Palatinate, one of Bavaria's non-contiguous territories located to the west along the Rhine.

Especially in Franconia, which had suffered grievously during the war Bavaria had just lost to Prussia, there was a great deal of ill feeling toward the government in Munich and the failed strategies in both the political and military arenas. For once, the ministers found an ally in the king's confidant, Richard Wagner. When Ludwig finally determined to undertake a journey of state, he wrote to the composer, "I desire once and for all to scatter the shadows of meanness, the clouds of ill-will and misinformation, that people often busily attempt to spread about me; I desire my people to experience what I really am and finally begin to truly know their prince."

> He doesn't want to; he would rather live in his dream world, in Wagnerism; he doesn't like the white-washed virgins who participate in ceremonies.
>
> *Eduard von Bomhard*
> *on Ludwig's dislike*
> *of tours of state*

Wagner's answer came swiftly. He expressed confidence that "among the friendly Franconian populace, everything will ultimately prove to be much better than among the cold-blooded, priest-driven masses of Munich. In the area around Bayreuth His Majesty will finally find his choice royal residence and—in the course of time—might move the entire government to this German heartland." With a play on the original meaning of the name of "Munich," Wagner promised that the "mastersingers" of Bayreuth would entice the king "away from his 'monk-residence' of Munich into the fresh, free air of Franconia." From Würzburg, the king wrote to Cosima von Bülow, wife of the renowned director Hans von Bülow, who now was Wagner's companion, "I firmly believe that in Nuremberg even the common people are more intelligent and good-willed than [in Munich] ...; here [Wagner's opera] *The Mastersingers* will catch fire. ... If I have any further reason to be dissatisfied with the inhabitants of my former capital city, nothing will prevent me from setting up my court in Nuremberg and transferring the seat of my government there."

The king set out on what was to be his only "great Franconian journey" on November 10, 1886, with an entourage of 119 men. He left Munich by way of Landshut and Regensburg for Bayreuth, a city which he had already visited at the age of seven with his parents and his brother, Otto. After the loss of the War of 1866, it was extremely important that the king make an appearance before the people of Bayreuth—for during the Prussian occupation many of the inhabitants had openly sympathized with the enemy and even welcomed them with cheers. On the route from the train station to the New Castle, people lined the streets and cheered the king in spite of the streaming rain. In the Jägerstrasse, today Bahnhofstrasse, 25

To find one's happiness in that
  of others
Is the joy of earthly life.
To be the source of others'
  well-being
Creates a divine satisfaction.
  Ludwig's entry in the poetry album
    of a young girl in Würzburg

young maids of honor, clad in white and blue, stood by the Gate of Honor; one of them recited a poem.

The king behaved very sociably the following day, attending a mass in the castle church in normal dress. At a midday dinner in the presence of fifty guests, and later at the ball in the evening in the "People's Hall," Ludwig took the hearts of his subjects by storm and danced "six turns" with the ladies of Bayreuth.

The next day, Ludwig visited Fasanerie Castle and then, in the uniform of a field marshal, mounted a horse to review the troops of the 7th Infantry and 6th Cavalry Regiments—all the while receiving the cries of the crowd, "Long live the King!" Ludwig honored the mayor with the First Class Order of St. Michael and awarded a captain a golden watch for his courage. Wounded soldiers each received a ducat with the king's image.

Last but not least, the king visited the most important industries of the region, the cotton mill and the sugar refinery. Recalling that in 1851, when he had visited the factory as a young prince, the workers had presented him with a sugar loaf, he now thanked them with a donation of 100 guilders to the workers' funds for illness and social support. In the Margravian Opera House, which had been illuminated with gas for the first time in honor of the royal visit, the "Dilettante Musicians Club" gave a concert. At the conclusion of the *Jubilatio Overture* by Carl Maria von Weber, the curtain was opened to reveal a bust of the king surrounded by genii and illuminated by a kind of fireworks. Around 10:00 P.M., a great torch procession proceeded from Jean-Paul Square to the New Castle, where the king was presented with a serenade. From the balcony he thanked the people; his voice rising clearly and loudly above the falling rain, he expressed his

In each city the king visited, he was presented with poems composed in his honor. In Würzburg, a certain gentleman by the name of von Scharff-Scharffenstein rhymed a poem of four stanzas ending:
"O excellent scion of Wittelsbach, remember / That we proudly and loyally stand beside you, / And just as you are doing now, continue to give us the gift of your heart! / Command us once more to the battle, / We will never waver in our fidelity! / Long live King Ludwig, Duke of your Frankish subjects."

gratitude, "I give you my warmest and most heartfelt thanks".

The journey progressed on to Bamberg. In Schweinfurt the king felt unwell; in Kissingen he drove across the battlefield of July 10, 1866, under strong snow flurries. He then passed through Hammelburg and Aschaffenburg on his way to Würzburg, where he stayed in the former episcopal residence of the prince-bishop, which had been built by the architect Balthasar Neumann—Napoleon had termed it "the most beautiful parsonage in Germany." Wherever the king appeared, usually in dress uniform, the people honored him. In the military hospitals, every wounded soldier received a ducat with the king's image. In addition, he donated 10,000 guilders toward relief of the war damages in Franconia and another 10,000 guilders to the Union for the Support of Those Harmed by the War.

On November 29, Ludwig toured the battlefields of the 1866 German War on horseback. Üttingen was his first stop, where he lunched with Countess Karoline von Wolfskeel and awarded the mistress of the castle the Service Order of the Bavarian Crown for her particular efforts to see that the wounded were cared for during the fighting.

Ludwig then progressed across snow-covered paths to Helmstadt, where his cousin, who was later to wear the crown as Ludwig III, had been wounded. His visits to the military fields at Remlingen and Rossbrunn affected the king greatly, and he canceled the rest of the program in Würzburg on account of his nerves.

Without a doubt, the high point of the tour was Nuremberg. On November 30, 1866, the monarch sent a telegraph to Cosima von Bülow for Richard Wagner, using, as so often, aliases from one of the operas, here from the *Mastersingers*:

The journey was beautiful; all reports fulfilled themselves splendidly, and even the return to Munich was good. Now you understand why the "honorables" claim that Munich is not really Bavarian.   *Cosima von Bülow, from Basle, December 17, 1866*

19   "Nuremberg, Ville Imperiale ▶ en Franconie" (view of the Free Imperial City of Nuremberg). Colored copper engraving by Pieter van der Aa, 1729.

To Hans Sachs

Have arrived two hours ago, unequaled jubilation!
From here, we want to save Germany,
Here, where Sachs lived and Walther won the singing
   contest.
The insignificant works of the evil-minded sink into
   nothingness,
The dark forces did not win their deceptive game.
Through you it rises again, that which had, alas, sunken
   so deeply,
The once all-powerful German spirit.
Your breath ignites flames from the sparks,
Your magic word commands [the spirit] to rise again.
To you, who employed the "ecstasy" in your blessed
   work,
True greetings are sent today from Walther.
Walther von Stolzing

What most fascinated the king in his "beloved Nuremberg,
which daily becomes dearer to me," was the mastersinger Hans
Sachs; Ludwig even made a pilgrimage to the place on which

his house had stood. The city enthralled him to such an extent that on December 5, he bade his brother Otto to come as well. Together they made a short excursion to Erlangen and on the following day visited the German National Museum. In addition, they viewed the Lenz iron casting works and the school of commercial arts. During his visits to the various factories, including one to the Zeltner ultramarine dye works, the king left money that was to be distributed among the workers.

Although it initially had been difficult to stir Ludwig's enthusiasm for this journey through Franconia, he became increasingly more companionable. Even at the balls that were given in his honor, which he generally did not enjoy, he comported himself as a gallant and consummate cavalier toward the ladies. As the king finally emerged and became visible, the populace responded enthusiastically toward their monarch, whose good looks and youth won approval everywhere.

The French journeys

In all, King Ludwig made three journeys to France: the first in 1867 to the Paris International Exhibition, then in 1874 to Paris and Versailles, and finally in 1875 to Rheims.

From a political standpoint, each of the journeys was a great mistake. In 1867, the French newspaper *La Situation* went so far as to call the visit of the Bavarian monarch "an event of incalculable political resonance." After all, Bavaria had just lost a war with Prussia, which naturally feared that the king might be making overtures to France. In fact, however, his reason for the trip was "merely not to omit anything that might help the position of Bavaria." Furthermore, Ludwig wanted to visit the International Exhibition, which was

In February 1848, a revolt broke out in France against the system of restoration that had been established after the defeat of Napoleon. Paris in particular was the scene of conflicts at the barricades and massive riots by radical socialists, soon joined by the bourgeois elements. The "Citizen King" Louis-Philippe was forced to resign, and **Louis Napoleon Bonaparte** won the presidential elections with 74 percent of the vote. After a coup in December 1851, he had himself crowned "Emperor of the French by the Grace of God and the Will of the Nation." He recognized the significance of socio-economic developments and

probably the most exciting event of the day. On the evening of July 20, Ludwig rode from Berg Castle to Gauting, where he departed in a special train for Paris. Accompanying him were Ludwig's Adjutant General von der Tann; his Adjutant Sauer; his private secretary Brochier; Cabinet Treasurer Grünwalt; and of course the cabinet secretary, along with three servants and a hairdresser.

In Hôtel du Rhin, Ludwig met his grandfather, King Ludwig I, and on July 22, the young monarch visited the Tuileries and met with Napoleon III. At the time, the

20   Napoleon III and Empress Eugénie. Photograph.

emperor's wife, Eugénie—famed for her beauty, but not especially liked for her political influence on the country—was in England, but Ludwig made her acquaintance four weeks later in the reception hall of the Augsburg train station.

Ludwig received preferred treatment. Of the many emperors and kings staying in Paris at the time, Napoleon personally accompanied only the Bavarian monarch and the king of Portugal to the agricultural sector of the exhibit. They also attended the operas *Don Carlos*, *The African*, *Mignon*, and *Romeo and Juliet* at the Grand Opéra together.

On July 24, Napoleon III invited Ludwig on an excursion to Compiègne and the nearby castle Pierrefonds, where a

attempted to address the social problems that followed in their wake through large-scale unemployment programs. Initially, he took an authoritarian position against the increasing democratic opposition, but in 1860 had to acquiesce to liberalization. During the so-called Second Empire, France was marked by strong nationalist feelings and a desire for national prestige. As a result, in 1870 Napoleon III allowed himself to be drawn into war with Prussia against his better judgment. After the French defeat in the Sudan, he was captured and dethroned. He died in 1873 in English exile.

heavily symbolic—but ultimately insignificant—scene was played out. Within the framework of a parade of hussars, a historical event dating from 757 was re-enacted, in which the Bavarian duke, Tassilo III, had been forced to swear numerous oaths of vassalage to the Frankish ruler.

In a letter to Cosima von Bülow, Ludwig reported that he had spent six to seven hours on the grounds of the world fair without tiring. Nonetheless, he stated that he would be glad to leave Paris soon, that modern Babylon with its pleasure-loving people, its horrible language, and hellishly ridiculous spectacles. "O for a refreshing rest after the days of haste in the mad rush of the world!"

Ludwig's desire to visit the palace at Versailles remained unfulfilled. His uncle Otto, who had at one time been King of Greece, died in Bamberg on July 26, 1867, and the young king set out at once to Bavaria, where he arrived at Berg Castle on July 29.

Not until his second French tour in 1874 did Ludwig succeed in visiting Versailles. On this trip, Ludwig quartered in the German Embassy with his former Prime Minister Chlodwig, Prince von Hohenlohe-Schillingsfürst.

By celebrating his 29th birthday in Versailles, the king succeeded in annoying both Munich and Paris. The Bavarians were angry that he had not come home for the occasion, while the French were agitated by the fact that in the person of Ludwig a German sovereign was once again on French soil, so soon after the French defeat in the War of 1870 and the imperial declaration in Versailles. Ludwig, however, traveling under the name of a count of Berg, did not allow himself to be diverted from his aim, not even by a report of the cholera epidemic raging in Paris. Finally Otto von Bismarck, chancellor and power behind the throne in the newly unified

Germany, intervened and granted Ludwig "permission" for his visit.

At 11 o'clock on the day of his birthday, the fountains at the park of the Versailles palace were turned on just for the king—a spectacle involving a cost of 50,000 francs, paid for by the French treasury. French newspapers commented in unison that "Mr. Bismarck," who had already obtained a great deal of money from France in reparations for the war, really ought to have covered the expenses himself.

Ludwig spent two days and a night in Versailles, then traveled on to Fontainbleau. In Paris he visited the Louvre, and reverently stood a long while before Napoleon's tomb in the Church of the Invalids. Ludwig did not meet the president of the French republic, Maurice MacMahon, Duke of Magenta; on the other hand, his French tour provided him with many new ideas for castle-building.

A year later, the king once more fled celebrations of his birthday in Munich for a more intimate circle gathered in

22   The fountain display in Versailles, created in honor of King Ludwig II's 29th birthday. Photograph c. 1890.

◀ 21   Private lounge car used by Ludwig II for his travels.

Rheims. As earlier, his travel plans were kept strictly secret, and Ludwig once again was accompanied by Stable Master Count Holnstein and the General Director of the Bavarian Railway Schamberger. At the German-French border station at Avricourt near Lúneville, three wagons provided by the government in Paris stood ready. Whereas Ludwig rarely allowed himself to be seen by the populace in Munich, he went for a stroll through Rheims on the very evening of his arrival. On the following day, he visited the gothic cathedral of Notre Dame, the old coronation hall, and the church of Saint Rémi. To his annoyance, the king was soon recognized; he ordered the baggage to be packed and returned to Castle Hohenschwangau. To his mother he wrote that the dear, venerable city of Rheims had please him "highly."

Journeys to Switzerland

On October 18, 1865, a performance of Friedrich Schiller's *William Tell* in the court theater spurred Ludwig to embark on a two-week tour of Switzerland, though he did not follow through on his original intention of taking one of the actors along with him. Instead, he traveled incognito with a very small entourage to Lucerne, where he stayed at the hotel Schweizer Hof. His next station was the rural inn Rössli in Brunnen, which he used as a base for visiting the various locations of the Tell saga—Tell's plateau, the Stauffacher chapel, and Rütli, where according to legend 33 men had sworn on November 7, 1307, to overthrow the Austrian tyranny. Ludwig even visited the Hohle Gasse near Küssnacht.

Ludwig could not put the thought of William Tell out of his mind. In June 1881, Ludwig, now 35 years old, expressed

Friedrich Schiller (1759–1805) often dramatized the idea of freedom in his works. In an age that had to come to terms with the French Revolution, Schiller's plays (including *William Tell*, *The Robbers*, and *Wallenstein*) raised politically explosive ideas—although they were not always understood and acknowledged as such by his contemporaries. Not until the second half of the 19th century, after Schiller and Goethe had been accepted as the central figures of German classicism, was full attention given to Schiller's œuvre. By the beginning of the 20th century, he was acclaimed as the true German

the wish to visit Lake Vierwaldstätter once more. Originally he had appointed the actor Emil Rhode to accompany him, but subsequently replaced the forty-year-old actor with a younger man, the twenty-three-year-old Josef Kainz. The young, Hungarian-born actor had debuted in August 1880, and was allowed to play a role in a private performance for the king in the spring of 1881. On April 30, he played Didier from Victor Hugo's *Marion de Lorme* before Ludwig, who was so fascinated that he had the performance repeated on May 4 and 10. In addition, the king "royally" rewarded Kainz with gifts. The young actor received a sparkling ring of sapphires and diamonds, a golden chain with a symbolic swan, and a diamond-encrusted watch. Ultimately, the actor was permitted to lodge in the guest quarters during two subsequent private showings.

These were not the only honors the young actor, already so "royally" recognized, was to receive. One morning, Kainz was suddenly called from the rehearsal of William Shakespeare's *Richard III* into the administrative office, where he found the Master of the Stables Karl Hesselschwerdt awaiting him with a summons to visit the king at Linderhof castle for three days.

On May 30, the lonely king received the actor in the grotto after dark. The next day, they proceeded to Hunding's hut, and on June 1 Lake Plan. The following third day took them into the Graswang Valley. Ludwig described the visit extensively in his diary:

national poet, but the swift dissolution of idealistic thought brought about by the economic and scientific developments of the new century relegated Schiller's art to the realms of rhetoric and pathos.

23   Hunding's hut (from Richard Wagner's opera *The Valkyrie*, the second one in the *Götterdämmerung* cycle), detail. Watercolor.

"Table at the linden (*Bride of Messina*) to the Moroccan House, coffee, listened to that heavenly voice again (*Don Carlos*), grotto illumination. ..." The phrase "table at the linden" refers to a linden tree with a wide crown in the castle park at Linderhof, under which Ludwig had a bower made to dine or chat with chosen guests.

The king and the actor were constantly underway until June 6. At Brunnenkopf, Kainz had to recite from Calderon's *Phaeton*, at Pürschling, passages from *Tell*. Upon their return to Oberammergau, they dined together and then returned in the dusk to Linderhof. Pentecost offered opportunity for a short stroll, private hours together, and another drive through the Graswang Valley—this time with a very lively recitation from *The Decameron*. Ultimately, in the grotto, Kainz received a specially designed and highly ornate cup, called the dream cup. The actor did not return to Munich until Whitmonday. The king had suggested that they address each other with *du*, the intimate form of "you" adopted only by family members and close friends—a very unusual token of familiarity from a Bavarian monarch. Ludwig was extraordinarily taken with the actor, referring to him as a true friend. The king wanted to take a journey with him, so that the actor could experience the lands in which Schiller's dramas were set. The monarch had a long-standing wish to visit Spain to follow the trail of *Don Carlos*, and then to return to Switzerland in memory of *Wiliam Tell*. Although the idea of a Spanish journey fell by the way-side, the trip to Switzerland did in fact materialize.

Kainz had difficulty with the amount of confidence the king placed in him. He dared to tell the king that he was moody, for example, and criticized him for slapping his servants, and held it to be ignoble when the king behaved un-kindly. Ludwig, however, forbade such criticism.

24 View of Lake Urner, looking ▶
toward Rütli, Tell's chapel, Tell's
plain, Altdorf, and Seelisberg.

The legendary journey through Switzerland began on June 27, 1881. Ludwig was accompanied by Kainz, six court officials, six chamber servants, and two personal cooks. Without any necessity, the king bore a passport with a pseudonym, the "Marquis de Saverny," whereas Kainz was given one under the name "Didier", both of whom were characters from *Marion de Lorme*.

The first station at Axenstein Castle had more guests than pleased the king—in fact, it appeared like a regular hotel. He fled away and rented the magnificently situated and well-protected Villa Gutenberg, where the king and the actor spent two weeks.

On several occasions the pair visited the Rütli House, but never before evening, long after the numerous tourists had left.

Ludwig also dispatched the actor to climb the Suren Pass above Altdorf and the ruins of Attinghausen. He was supposed to spend the night in Engelberg and hike the following day over the Joch Pass to Melchthal, where Ludwig would await him. The king looked forward to the romanticism of the scene Kainz was to recite Schiller's verses from *William Tell* upon his arrival:

Through the fearsome mountains of the Suren,
Across the wide and barren fields of ice,
Where only the hoarse voice of the lammergeier crows,
I made my way to the Alpentrift,
Where the shepherds from Uri and Engelberg
Call to each other in greeting and share the meadows.

At his side, Kainz, who had never before climbed a mountain, was now to clamber up to the summit of Suren—along with four strong companions, a great deal of food, and a dozen bottles of champagne. With very sore feet, the group did not reach the guest house Sonnenblick in Engelberg, where they were supposed to sleep, until after midnight. The next day, no power on earth was great enough to motivate Kainz to continue the journey.

The king, rather annoyed, waited futilely at Melchthal, but finally returned to the lake, where Kainz also finally showed up—riding in a wagon. Ludwig was deeply disappointed when Kainz termed his hike horrible. In place of the original hike, the king now proposed that on the following night they should climb to the summit of the Rütli, where the actor was to recite the Melchthal tale. They embarked the next evening in the 130-foot-long steamer *Waldstätter*, which was being maintained under steam 24 hours a day in readiness for the king on Lake Vierwaldstätter. Although Kainz was tired, the king wanted to hear 14 alphornists, who were supposed to present the *Kuhreigen* tune during the cruise. Kainz found the horns far too loud, but nonetheless fell asleep, snoring out loud. The king disembarked and climbed Rütli alone.

A week later, affairs finally ground to a halt. On July 11, the king dragged the young man up Rütli at 2:00 A.M. Ludwig reveled in the moonlight on the snow-covered peaks in the

Josef Kainz (born January 2, 1858, in Wisselburg, Hungary; died September 20, 1910, Vienna) came to the Burgtheater in Vienna in 1899 following engagements in Munich and Berlin. He is credited with founding a modern, psychologically oriented approach to drama, and was respected in his own age as the greatest German actor. His admirers praised his sensibility and the poetry of his acting, as well as his wonderful voice: "He spoke as the wind blows through an aeolian harp—sharply, lamentingly, excitedly, movingly moved."

mild summer night and asked the actor to begin with the Melchthal scene. Kainz spoke not a work. The king made a second request to begin; he ordered; he demanded. But Kainz was too tired; he laid himself on the grass and instantaneously fell asleep. Furious, Ludwig left him where he lay and started his return to Villa Gutenberg. After Kainz awakened, he followed the king back, overtook him on the way, and asked forgiveness.

Hiding his disappointment, the king took Kainz along in search of antique clocks for his collection. It was at this point that he hit upon the idea of having himself photographed together with the actor. The result was two truly unusual photographs. The king had long lost his slim figure, a fact which he attempted to hide with a large and heavy winter coat. In one picture, the king is sitting on the chair with the

25   Ludwig II with Josef Kainz at the end of their journey on the trail of William Tell. The lack of harmony between them is clearly evident.

actor standing at his side; in the other the positions are re-versed.

The journey reached its end shortly thereafter. Together the pair rode in Ludwig's parlor wagon to the border. From there Kainz traveled on to Munich alone, while the king returned to Linderhof. At the moment of parting, the king gave Kainz a hearty embrace. In spite of the tensions of the journey, for Ludwig, this leave-taking was synonymous with a return to his isolation. Nonetheless, the king was irritated enough to cancel the private performance of Victor Hugo's *Les Burgraves*, in which Kainz was to play Ottbert. Still unsatisfied, Ludwig then reconsidered and sent Kainz a painting of Lake Vierwaldstätter as a gift. Kainz, however, returned the painting.

After some time, Kainz was once again allowed to appear in private showings. He played Rustan in Grillparzer's *The Dream of Life*—a theme idea with which Ludwig could well identify. Just as the contact with the actor was about to be renewed, however, the king let it be known that he never wanted to hear the actor's name again. Instead Kainz received an engagement with the German Theater in Berlin, where he successfully debuted as Ferdinand in Schiller's *Love and Cabals* on September 29, 1883. In November of the same year, he triumphed as Don Carlos. In addition to his undisputed dramatic talent, the public's interest in the "playmate" of the Bavarian king may have contributed to his success in Berlin.

Ludwig and Women

Duchess Sophie Charlotte of Bavaria—the king's bride

"Do you want to be my wife?
Partner on my throne?"

Ludwig I enthused over his grandson: "You are a most fortunate man. No woman can resist you." At the same time, he also warned him not to settle down too quickly. "You know I mean well and therefore cannot help but express my heartfelt wish that you not yet commit yourself to marriage. At your age, you are much too young to get married yet, and since you have grown a little too fast, it would be harmful to your health. Before you make a commitment, give yourself the freedom to meet a number of princesses so that you can make a choice. With time, many things appear in a different light than on first impression. It is a matter of the happiness of your whole family for the rest of your life. Therefore do not rush, but maintain a free hand! This is my conviction, my dear grandson, your grandfather Ludwig who adores you and wishes you only the best."

Ludwig had great affection for his cousin Elisabeth, who was eight years older and had been married to Emperor Francis Joseph of Austria since 1854. They shared a love for everything beautiful and mystical, as well as a profound dislike of formal obligations at court. They both felt uncomfortable in large social gatherings at the court and hated to be the

Oh, women! Even the most intelligent of them disputes without logic.
Ludwig II commenting on women, according to a letter of the theologian Ignaz Döllinger to his friend Charlotte von Leyden

26 Ludwig II's favorite cousin, Empress Elisabeth of Austria, a daughter of Grand Duke Maximilian of Bavaria. Copy by E. Riegele (1923) of a painting by Franz Xaver Winterhalter, 1864.

center of attention. Over the years they both withdrew more and more from the public, became very lonely and felt misunderstood.

Very gradually, Ludwig became attracted to Elisabeth's youngest sister, Sophie Charlotte. Her parents, Grand Duke Maximilian of Bavaria and his wife, Grand Duchess Ludovika, daughter of Maximilian I Joseph and Caroline of Bavaria, maintained residences both in the Bavarian capital Munich and at their summer palace in Possenhofen on Lake Starnberg.

In his love letters to his bride, Ludwig II repeatedly invited Sophie Charlotte and her mother to have dinner with him in the enchanting winter garden at his residence in Munich. He sent flower bouquets, presents and letters, so much so that the grand duchess felt obliged to speak to the queen mother out of concern for her daughter's reputation. She did not wish to have her called the "king's playmate." When the queen mother asked her son about his intentions, he decided with surprising swiftness to ask for Sophie's hand. Thus, on the night of January 22, 1867, after attending a ball, Ludwig wrote Sophie a letter in which he proposed marriage: "Do you want to be my wife, partner of my throne, Queen of Bavaria?" Nearly bursting with excitement, the young king

27 Engagement announcement ▶ of Ludwig II and Sophie of Bavaria, the youngest sister of Empress Elisabeth of Austria, January 1867.

came to his mother's bedchamber at dawn and informed her
of his intention, and asked her to obtain the consent of
Sophie's parents. This was not difficult for the queen mother
because she had herself maintained a very cordial relationship with the duchess from the time she had come to Munich
as a young princess. The following day, confirmation arrived
from Possenhofen. On the evening of the engagement, King
Ludwig attended a performance at the Residence Theater.
Queen Marie asked the duchess to join the royal box and
Sophie took her seat next to the king, applauded by the enthusiastic audience.

They made a handsome couple. The king, still a tall, slender young man with expressive dark eyes, was an impressive
figure in the uniform of his calvary regiment, and with the
tall, slim bride wearing an attractive blue-and-white ball gown
embroidered with silver stars, they were charming to behold.
Engagement photographs could be admired in all store windows throughout Munich. The Royal Mint issued a memorial
coin in honor of the event, while the king ordered a magnificent wedding carriage and had the so-called garden suite in
the residence restored for his future queen. It was also the
king's desire that Wagner's opera *The Mastersingers of Nuremberg* be performed as part of their marriage celebration. Even
if some "shortsighted people consider the work unsuitable for
a wedding, I will not be irritated," he declared.

J. ALBERT K. HOFPHOTOGRAPH IN MÜNCHEN

Ludwig immediately informed his grandfather of his engagement to Sophie. We know his commentary, "… happy that he gets married. That Sophie loves him is obvious from the way she looks at him. But will it be a happy marriage? She has not the same independence of mind as her sisters?" He was referring to Sophie's sisters Helene, since 1858 wife of Hereditary Prince Maximilian Anton Lamoral of Thurn and Taxis; Elisabeth (Sisi), Empress of Austria; Marie, wife of Francis II, King of both Sicilies; and Mathilde, who was married to Ludwig, Prince of Bourbon-Sicily, Count Trani. Born in 1847, Sophie was the youngest of the grand duke's daughter, a very attractive young woman of slender build, with a pretty face and opulent ash-blond hair that she wore braided on top of her head.

What role did the two mothers play after the engagement? According to Ludwig's letter to Sophie of January 27, 1867, his mother told him of a concern that the mother of the bride had confided to her that evening after the theater: Sophie had told a lady-in-waiting that Ludwig did not truly love her. The king wrote, "But dear Sophie, do you really doubt that I love with all my heart? I am sorry, I am truly sorry. I hope your mother simply misunderstood something. What am I to believe? Good night now, my dearest Sophie, a thousand warm greetings, your faithful Ludwig." The following day, Ludwig wrote once more that he would "never be led into confusion by our mothers' gossip. I am wondering, however, why our mothers constantly interfere and gossip. How annoying and upsetting."

In February, an engagement ball was held in the royal residence. The king, who obviously was not having a good time, quietly bade Prince Hohenlohe to check his watch unobtrusively, for Ludwig did not want to miss the performance

28   Possenhofen Castle at Lake Starnberg, the summer residence of the Dukes of Bavaria. Detail of an 1864 gouache.

of one of Schiller's dramas that night—or at least hoped to catch the end of it. When there proved still to be time, he secretly left the party without even taking leave of his bride. His guests were not at all pleased with his behavior; Sophie herself was certainly annoyed, but not really alarmed. Ludwig had always been unconventional and unpredictable. He used to show up at the Possenhofen palace unannounced at midnight, for example, causing considerable discontent because a lady-in-waiting had to be present at their nocturnal meetings and observe them from behind an ivy bower. The king would gently kiss Sophie on the forehead; often he would not talk at all for half an hour or just say "you have wonderful eyes" while Sophie continued working on her boring embroidery.

One great passion united Sophie and Ludwig, however. They both adored Richard Wagner. Inspired by his opera *Lohengrin*, Ludwig began to call his bride Elsa. He himself, though, did not identify with the figure of Lohengrin, who wed Elsa of Brabant, but rather with Heinrich, modeled upon the German King Henry the Fowler. In the opera, Heinrich presided over the court at Antwerp, where he functioned as a fair judge. Sophie, who was an excellent pianist and singer, tried to please the king by singing the arias of Elsa, Elisabeth, and Senta.

In December 1866, the king sent Richard Wagner cordial greetings from his "cousin" Sophie through Cosima von Bülow, who recalled that she had often noticed the presence of "Her Royal Highness" at concerts in Munich. On January 3, 1867, Cosima inquired, "Would she be a proper soul mate for the Precious Loner?" A mere two days later he replied, "I shall let Sophie know the friend (Richard Wagner) appreciated her greetings. It will make her very happy. I have

My dear Elsa!
My warmest thanks for your dear letter yesterday. I can assure you, the doubts expressed at the end of your note are completely unfounded. Of all the women in the world, you are most dear to me. ... [H]owever, as you well know, the God of my life is Richard Wagner.

Ludwig II to Sophie of Bavaria,
responding o letters in which
she questions his love for her

hardly any opportunity to see her; we correspond occasionally; the faithful, devoted Count Holnstein is the messenger of our letters. ... Sophie is a devoted, compassionate, and sensitive soul whose fate slightly resembles mine, as we are both surrounded by people who do not understand us and judge us wrongly; we live as if we were in an oasis of the desert."

Ludwig confided to Cosima he loved his bride "faithfully and truly" and he hoped that the two women would get to know each other soon. In great secrecy, Sophie met with Richard Wagner in Munich. In Possenhofen Wagner was considered a persona non grata. The meeting was therefore arranged in the house of Sophie's brother, Duke Ludwig, at 22 Kanalstrasse in Munich. Richard Wagner very much liked the idea of the duchess as future queen.

After their engagement, the couple met only rarely, and the king's intentions began to waver. He still spoke about "longing to get married," but also claimed he had no time to do so. He wrote to Otto that his brother really ought to fulfill the dynastic obligations, but added, "If it is at all possible that there is a woman who could make me happy, it would be Sophie and no other." He borrowed the queen's crown from the Royal Treasury to place it on Sophie's head so that it could be adjusted to fit. During their engagement, Ludwig planned a trip to Rome with his mother that did not materialize. He went to Eisenach with his brother instead, and from there continued on alone to visit the International Exhibition in Paris.

A letter from Sophie's mother, the Duchess Ludovika, at the beginning of March indicates that the couple did not often attend the balls because Ludwig did not enjoy dancing. The pair might meet at dinners, however, and when she, Ludo-

My esteemed Friend, precious Sir!
It is impossible to express my heartfelt congratulations that you have found an understanding, loving, beloved wife for which I have prayed from the depths of my soul—you have found a wife who understands you! This year is thrice blessed. ... I have nothing else to add. Your happiness, my dear Highness, will tell you how deeply we share your joy. I remain your ever true and grateful friend.
Letter of Cosima von Bülow from Tribschen, January 24, 1867

vika, could not be present as chaperone, then the couple was left to the protection of the queen, that is, of Sophie's future mother-in-law, Marie.

A wedding date was initially set for August 1867. Ludwig II postponed it once to October 12, the wedding day of both his parents and his grandparents, and then once again to November 28. The bride's parents were outraged. Duchess Ludovika wrote to the queen mother on September 27, 1867, "You will surely understand that these postponements of the wedding date make us feel very uncomfortable and doubtful. Remarks that have been made by the king's men have underscored my concerns. They have leaked that King would rather marry in a few years, that he feels he is still too young to commit himself, that he wants to enjoy his freedom, and even that it would be better to cause Sophie to break the engagement. A few days ago, she did this and returned his promise in writing to him. He did not accept it, but instead confirmed the date of the ceremony for the end of November instead of the day of December 1, as originally planned."

A few days later, on October 4, 1867, the grand duchess sent another note in which she wrote, "The repeated postponements of the wedding date make us feel very uneasy and have caused annoying gossip. Max felt obliged to write a note to the

29   Ludwig II and his fiancée Sophie, Duchess of Bavaria. Photograph by Joseph Albert, 1867.

king telling him that such behavior is no longer in keeping with Sophie's honor. He asked the king to either stick to the end of November date or to consider his request for Sophie's hand, which he had made a full eight months ago, as rejected. Max certainly does not want to pressure the king to keep his promise. But it has never been our intention to force our daughter on him."

The duke's ultimatum infuriated the king. Ludwig was of the opinion that the duke was simply a "subject like any other" and that he had no right to write to his king in such a tone. In a short note he addressed to Sophie, Ludwig even made her father responsible for their conflicts: "Beloved Elsa! Your brutal father wants to separate us. Always yours, Heinrich."

On October 5, 1867, the Queen Mother Marie wrote a letter to her son from Berchtesgaden: "Just back from Salzburg, I found a letter from Aunt Louise (Sophie's mother, Ludovika) and am anxious to know what you will answer Duke Max. God bless your reply." Ludwig decided to break off his engagement!

The king justified his decision in a very detailed letter to his "dear and precious friend" Cosima von Bülow and confided to her his most intimate thoughts. Confirming once again his affection for Sophie, he also admitted that his love was not strong enough to make her his wife and queen. The future seemed shrouded in darkness and he felt this marriage would rob him of every opportunity to find happiness. "If within a year, the person destined to me by God should appear and if I were attracted to her by a love that I would have to fulfill, how very unhappy I would have become! Everything would have been too late. I would have had to sacrifice myself to Sophie whom I married." He still intended

"I love you so much, my dear Edgar. While I am with you I cannot really express to you how deeply your precious image rests in my heart, so deep, that I shamefully forget my obligations towards my poor king," wrote **Sophie** on July 23, 1867, to the photographer Edgar Hanfstaengl. Sophie's later life proved a very difficult path. She married Ferdinand von Orléans, Duke of Alençon, lived in England, Palermo, Naples, Rome, Possenhofen and—after 1871—Vincennes. She had an affair with the Austrian physician Dr. Glaser and fled with him to Meran in northern Italy. Due to pressure from Empress Elisabeth,

to marry one day, but he felt too young and wanted to have enough time "to find the person destined to me by God." Although it was difficult for him to compromise Sophie's position, he opted for his freedom. " I only long for freedom, freedom, for freedom I thirst."

Cosima congratulated him on his decision to break the engagement. She held that Sophie's family, the Max family—as the Bavarian people referred to them—was not popular, but rather very powerful and ill-willed. She felt certain that they only wanted to take advantage of the king's decision to break the engagement. Finally, she wrote, "I am truly sorry for Princess Sophie alone. If she loves you she will accept your decision. If she does not—then she, too, must be relieved to be free."

In fact, the latter was true. During the official photography sessions for the engagement, Sophie had fallen in love with the photographer Edgar Hanfstaengl. They had exchanged love letters, which were discovered some years ago. It is highly unlikely that Ludwig II ever knew of his bride's affair.

On October 11, 1867, a government bulletin announced the dissolution of the royal marriage plans with the following words: "The engagement of his Royal Highness the King with Princess Sophie has been canceled by mutual agreement because they have come to the conclusion that they do not share the true attraction of hearts on which a happy marriage is based."

All Bavaria—and not only Bavaria—had looked forward to the announced wedding. Wherever the fiancés had appeared together, people were delighted. Ludwig and Sophie made a true fairytale couple. All the newspapers noted that Sophie would be the first queen of Bavaria who was both

---

her sister, she was locked away in the private insane asylum Maria Grün near Graz, Austria, until she agreed to give up Dr. Glaser. In Paris, she entered the Third Order of the Dominicans under the name Sister Marie Madeleine. In 1897, she organized a charity bazaar in her monastery.

Fire broke out and she was burned beyond recognition in the flames.

On October 8, Ludwig II poured out his soul to his "dear, precious friend" Cosima von Bülow in a very telling and detailed letter informing her of the reasons he broke off his engagement:

Now that the decision has been made, my tortures have dissolved and it is good; I am calm and serene; the peace that I had lost has returned to my soul and shall, as I firmly believe and certainly hope, never leave me again. ... Since I know that you, my dearly loved and loyal friend, share my happiness and my sorrows truly and compassionately, I will follow the impulse of my soul once more and empty my heart, which you have always tended with great care. ... When I began to write my cousin Sophie frequently last summer, enthusiastically sharing my thoughts with her about our great friend and master, whom I adore and love, and when I began to send her books, letters, etc., her mother found out about our correspondence. In her naïve and clumsy way, she mistook them for ordinary love letters. This dragon did not understand that we were sharing a purely spiritual relationship. Like all such limited people do, she measured sublimity with a limited scale. ... Sophie's affection for me was true love; she was devastated to find out that I did not love her equally. Out of deep feelings and true compassion for her sorrow, I hastily and without enough reflection proposed marriage to her. ... I have known her since my youth and have always loved my dear cousin truly and tenderly as a sister; I gave her my confidence and my friendship but not my love. You can imagine how terrible I felt when—as the wedding date came closer and closer— I realized that this bond would not be happy for either of us. It was very difficult to make it all undone. "I only long for freedom, freedom, for freedom I thirst." I pulled away, not wanting to run blindly into a disaster. I am still so young and have much time to find the being who is destined for me by God. Why would I tie myself in marriage to someone who, as a close relative, I have always loved but not so much that I would make her my queen, my wife. The future seems shrouded in darkness. Why would I cut off any opportunity to become happy? If within a year, the person destined to me by God should appear and if I were attracted to her by a love that I would have to fulfill, how very unhappy I would have become! Everything would have been too late. I would have had to sacrifice myself to Sophie whom I married. It must be a terrible fate to be sacrificed. ... I had to fend off the threatening storm disaster that I had brought upon myself. I thought it was better to act immediately and explained everything to Sophie in a detailed letter. The engagement canceled; she is free; she can still find happiness and so can I.

What would have happened to all our plans if the disastrous marriage had taken place, if inner suffering, sorrow and grief had torn

Bavarian and Catholic after a succession of three Protestant queens. This wedding would have surpassed all previous festivities and would have been celebrated with "all Bavarian-Baroque pomp and ceremony."

But the extent to which Ludwig detested the thought of marriage to Princess Sophie is clear from a remark in a letter to Cosima von Bülow: "If it had not been possible to cancel our engagement by mutual agreement, I was determined to end my life by taking hydrocyanic acid." The king felt relieved to no longer be connected to Possenhofen and its inhabitants. "We did not belong together; I am glad I got rid of her." Five years later, on July 5, 1872, Cosima noted in her diary, "In Munich's beer halls people discuss openly that the

me apart? How would I have found the energy to pursue our ideals with enthusiasm? My golden dreams would have dissipated like idle fantasies. The School of Art would not have been established, there would have been no Festival Theater, the *Mastersingers* would not have existed for me, I would not have enjoyed the Nibelungen, Parsifal. I would have been a shadow who on this earth, would have led a dreary life without peace and excitement. A tenfold death would have been welcome pleasure. Everything, everything will be well now; I have awakened from a terrifying dream. I sense my former heroic strength returning to me, which must not betray its great destiny. Hail Wagner, for you I joyfully sacrifice the very last drop of my blood. Do I have to tell you how extraordinarily happy the most recent performance of Lohengrin made me? It gave me the strength to cut off a relationship that had become annoying and limiting. O, this divine work always emanates miraculous power! I certainly hope to come to the performance of the *Mastersingers* at the beginning of February. How much I long for the biography to continue, oh please, please! … I am coming to life again! I begin to recognize it again, this beautiful world which I had lost. Heaven looks down on me, nature glows richly decked; inner peace, serene joy of life gives sorrow no chance; flowers blossom before my inner eye where reality (as just now) has only ice and snow. Magnificent Hohenschwangau is imbued by poetry although tonight my mother is expected, personified prose. … Disgusted I look at this handwriting, forgive me, paper and quill are impossible.

I send thousand greetings to my beloved friend! True to death!

Ludwig
Hohenschwangau, October 8, 1867

present king will be the last King of Bavaria unless he marries; they cannot fathom being ruled by the Luitpold family and become Prussian."

Ludwig's brother Otto wrote to his cousin Therese in a very detached tone about the engagement: "It is sad how things have developed between Ludwig and Sophie. As terrible as it is, perhaps it is better for them to part now than to live together unhappily. ..." Empress Elisabeth, Sophie's sister, was outraged at first, but this anger toward her royal cousin vanished quickly. There are indications that she would have liked to see her favorite daughter, Marie Valérie, who was born in 1868, become Ludwig's future wife. A letter of the queen mother to Ludwig in September 1880 reads, "Sisi sent you an image of Valérie. but I can imagine that you do not want to hear about her yet!"

Ludwig himself entered in his diary, "Sophie erased, the dark image fades. I long for freedom, I am thirsting for freedom after a painful nightmare."

Czarina Maria Alexandrovna of Russia

Ludwig II not only adored Elisabeth, the Empress of Austria, but also the Czarina Maria Alexandrovna of Russia, who had far greater influence on his understanding of the nature and the social obligations of kingship than Elisabeth. In a letter of July 19, 1865, to the Bavarian State Secretary Ludwig, Baron von der Pforten, Ludwig described what so greatly fascinated him about the czarina: "I wish you had met the czarina of Russia. This unusual woman is like a saint. An aura of purity emanates from her." He assured the czarina that no one—without exception—had ever left such a deep and lasting

Since you were convinced of your future unhappiness in a certain affair, I am pleased to hear that you have regained your promise.
Ludwig I regarding the cancellation of the engagement in October 1867

impression on him than she. In her presence and through her words he felt himself lifted and supported "as through the power of a sacrament."

The czarina was the youngest child born to Grand Duke Ludwig II of Hesse and on the Rhine and his wife Wilhelmine, princess of Baden. Having been born on August 8, 1824, Maria was 21 years older than Ludwig. In April 1841, at the age of 16, the Protestant Princess Maria had married Alexander II, then crown prince of Russia, and converted to the Russian Orthodox faith. Of her eight children with the czar, the crown prince and heir to the Russian throne, Nikolai, died when he was just 22 years old. In addition, Maria Alexandrovna suffered greatly from a case of tuberculosis that went undetected for years.

Ludwig II and the czarina shared several degrees of blood relationship. Ludwig's aunt, his mother's sister Elisabeth of Prussia, had married Prince Karl of Hesse, the czarina's brother. Ludwig and the czarina first met personally in the summer of 1864 in the Bavarian spa Kissingen, shortly after Ludwig's accession to the throne. In that year, a number of royalty had gathered to spend the summer vacations together, including the Austrian emperor with an entourage of 58, the Russian emperor with his three children and an entourage of 88, as well as King Karl I of Württemberg and his queen, Olga. As a recent successor to a throne, King Ludwig II and his brother Otto arrived in Kissingen with an entourage of 25 on June 18, 1864, to pay his respects to the high-ranking spa guests. Although Ludwig had intended to remain only a few days, he ended up staying four weeks. Because the czar and czarina had brought their only daughter along, rumors began to spread of a possible engagement between Ludwig II and the Royal Duchess Marie, who at the

Alexander II, the son of Czar Nicholas I and Czarina Maria Alexandrovna, was born on April 29, 1818, in Moscow. He ascended the throne after his father's death in 1855. In 1856, he ended the Crimean War, which completed the annexation of the Crimea begun in 1783.

time was only eleven years old. Ludwig, however, was completely infatuated with the czarina, whom he tenderly addressed as "my angel," "my Empress," even "my true mother" in his correspondence with her. The czarina protested vehemently against the latter appellation and bade him to be particularly attentive and friendly to his own mother, who, she pointed out, bore the difficult fate of having lost her husband so early.

After the czarina had left Kissingen, Ludwig returned to Munich for two weeks on July 15, but then rushed off to Schwalbach in the Taunus Mountains on July 29, 1864, where Maria Alexandrovna was receiving after-treatment. In the summer of 1868, she once again returned to the spa at Kissingen for treatment, and Ludwig traveled there to meet her. On August 8, he was allowed to celebrate her birthday alone with the czarina. Ludwig II extended an invitation to come and visit him in one of his castles at the conclusion of her spa treatments. On September 26, he met her in Passing, in the vicinity of Munich, and they continued together to Berg Castle. While the majority of the imperial entourage took quarters at an inn at Lake Starnberg, Ludwig, the czarina and five of her entourage traveled on the steamship *Tristan* to Berg Castle, which he had offered the empress as domicile for her short visit while he moved into one of the adjacent buildings. After a dinner on Rose Island—Maria Alexandrovna is said to have called it the most poetically romantic dinner she had ever enjoyed—Ludwig and his guest returned to Berg Castle aboard the *Tristan*, to the accompaniment of music played by a Bavarian regiment. The royals entered the castle, and when they stepped out on the balcony, it was the cue for the beginning of fireworks that has been chronicled by the early 20th-century writer, Oscar Maria Graf, and painted

The sea festival took place. It was unimaginable. The whole lake turned into a single field of fire. The royal raft gleamed like a fairy island in the middle of good five hundred swift, flower-decorated boats that were whizzing around with blinking lights. The best orchestras played selections from Wagner's operas alternately with wonderful gondola songs the whole night long. The fish spearing was a total success, and the help of the Dennerdoling farm received a silver cup from the king personally.

Oskar Maria Graf, "Chronicle of Flechting," 1925

by Josef Walter (see below). The castle and park were brightly illuminated and a magnificent display of fireworks rose up over the lake. The entire night through, the best orchestras played selections of Wagner's operas or Italian gondolier music.

The following day, September 27, the king and the czarina attended church services and once again took the steamship across Lake Starnberg to St. Heinrich and Rose Island. In Possenhofen they paid a visit to Duke Maximilian and Duchess Ludovika, the parents of Sophie of Bavaria, who at the time was engaged to be married to Ludwig.

When the czarina continued on her way to Italy, Ludwig accompanied her as far as Innsbruck in the Austrian Alps, and on her return, he met her in Kufstein on November 14, 1868. The following night, Richard Wagner's opera *The Mastersingers of Nuremberg* was performed in honor of the czarina,

30   Czarina Maria Alexandrovna's visit to Berg Castle, September 26, 1868. Painting by Josef Walter.

and on November 16, Ludwig saw her off at the Bavarian border near Nördlingen as she embarked on her further travels.

Ludwig greatly appreciated the intimate relationship with Maria Alexandrovna and when alone with her experienced the most "unforgettable hours, which influenced my entire life." Free from "annoying court people," they spoke in detail about many questions that afflicted his soul. From her he even accepted heavy criticism regarding his lifestyle. Although they were often "angel-like" reminders, she pointedly asked him to strengthen his relationship with his subjects, and especially to try to overcome his inclination toward seclusion. She implored him to summon his will power and strengthen the monarchy and the love of the traditional dynasty in the hearts of Bavarians. In a letter of April 1869, Ludwig promised her he would do his best to cultivate and strengthen the "good healthy core that, thank God, still existed in his people." After the Bavarian defeat by Prussia in the German War of 1866 (cf. p. 71ff.), Ludwig took advantage of his connections to the Russian court. He implored the czarina to influence the czar on his behalf "to support me and my country in the attempt to decrease the exorbitant reparations claimed by Prussia."

When in 1865, the czarina was struck by the hardest blow a mother can experience, the death of her son Nikolai, successor to the Russian throne, Ludwig was filled with deep compassion.

In the summer of 1878 Ludwig II made preparations to visit Russia and Moscow—an almost unthinkable enterprise in light of his strong aversion to travel. In fact, he had not yet even managed to pay a long overdue visit of respect to the so-called "hero-emperor," William I, in the capital of Prussia,

31   Czarina Maria Alexandrovna. Steel engraving by August Weger, ca. 1855.

Berlin. The itinerary for the Russian tour had been determined, but information about the outbreak of a pox epidemic that was raging in Warsaw in Poland as well as the sanitary conditions along the route had still to be gathered. This finally provided Cabinet Secretary Friedrich von Ziegler a welcome opportunity to thwart, and finally to put an end to, the king's travel plans.

Lila von Bulyorszky

The graceful and very talented Hungarian actress Lila von Bulyorszky celebrated the height of her career on the stages of the Munich theaters. Ludwig admired her in the role of Friedrich Schiller's *Maria Stuart* and identified the artist—as was his habit—with her role in the theater. The king ordered the court painter F. Heigl to do a watercolor of the actress in this role. After a particularly stirring performance of *Maria Stuart*, Ludwig had the All Saints Church opened at midnight in order to pray for the soul of the unfortunate queen of the Scots.

Lila von Bulyorszky resided in the Maximilianstrasse in Munich. In her bedroom opposite her bed hung a large photograph of the young King Ludwig clad in the robe of a Knight of St. George. The relationship between the pair, however, is best described as "ebb and tide." Often the king called the artist to Hohenschwangau in the middle of winter. At times, she re-

32   Lila von Bulyorszky as Mary Stuart. Photograph by Joseph Albert, presumably ca. 1866.

ceived the spontaneous order to leave Munich within only 24 hours, to which demand she responded that she was well aware of her rights. At other times, the king lay in a state of greatest turmoil at her feet, but then again, forbade her to perform in the theater. In his letters, he called her his "beloved friend" and showered her with infatuated and poetic homages. Her visits to Hohenschwangau or Rose Island were naturally supposed to be kept completely confidential.

Even during his engagement to Sophie, King Ludwig II secretly invited the actress to Rose Island. After dinner, he offered her his arm for a short walk across the little island, which was planted with 150,000 blossoming roses. But it had rained and the gravel paths were wet; her delicate shoes and the train of her silk dress were soiled. The king then plucked some roses with his own hand and presented them to the actress, who now even feared for her gloves. When the king noticed this, he took the roses from her and suggested replacing the flowers in another form. Lila von Bulyorszky, who was married and had four children, dreamt of jewelry. Instead and to her great disappointment, she received pressed flowers; her expenses for the royal visits and her travel costs were not reimbursed.

During a three-day visit in Hohenschwangau, Ludwig showed the actress the most interesting sights in the castle, among them his bedchamber which, to her surprise, was decorated with erotic paintings.

Ludwig did not always behave pleasantly toward the actress. Once he told his ministerial counselor Franz Leinfelder that she had forced herself on him with such intensity that he had to flee to a corner of the room. He told the actor Josef Kainz that she once fell at his feet in his sled. At the

After Richard had first sung a song for him,
The Bulyorszky woman finally succeeded
In singing him the right tune,
The chaste fellow has now fallen, just like the others ...

Servants' song making fun of the suspected relationship between Lila von Bulyorszky and Ludwig II

behest of his mother and the cabinet secretary, the king brought the nocturnal meetings to an end. They began instead a correspondence, with Ludwig addressing her as "Julia" and "Mary Stuart" and signing his letters "Romeo" or "Mortimer."

Gottfried von Böhm, a biographer of Ludwig II, visited the sevety-one-year-old actress, who confided that after the "incident," the queen mother had summoned her to Hohenschwangau to tell her that the king would never be moved to marry as long as she remained in Bavaria. She made the actress promise not to renew her contract at the theater after it ran out eighteen months later. Lila von Bulyorszky gave her word and was true to it.

Marie Dahn-Hausmann

The relationship between Ludwig and the actress Marie Dahn-Hausmann was of a very different nature. As crown prince he had initially seen her play Thekla in Friedrich Schiller's *Wallenstein*. Even then she instilled an "honest and true affection" in him, as he wrote. In 1875, he invited her and her husband for a brief visit in his newly acquired estate of Herrenchiemsee.

The king greatly enjoyed corresponding with the actress. They both despised anything "low" and he wrote, "Often a vehement rage and hate attacks me. Then I turn away in anger from the chaotic reality, which offers me little. Perhaps one day, when all ideals whose fire I so carefully cultivate have broken down, I shall make peace with this world. But— never wish for that! I want to remain an eternal mystery to myself and others. ..."

I have always understood Your Majesty's poetical inclination for the mountains, with their crevices, tumbling streams, waterfalls, moss-covered rocks, and narrow animal trails, but only now do I appreciate it completely. Here [in the mountains], one is truly closer to nature and farther from people. Here I even feel the shyness toward your Majesty that usually holds me back disappear. And if Rose Island were located in an Alpine lake-Berg Castle, but 10,000 feet above sea-level, my heart would beat faster.   *Lila von Bulyorszky to Ludwig II*

Marie Dahn-Hausmann survived the king by many years. After becoming an honorary member of the Münchener Hofbühne, a stage in Munich sponsored by the royal court, she died in March 1909.

33   Marie Dahn-Hausmann.
Photograph.

The Wars of 1866 and 1870
and Founding of the Empire in 1871

The German War: 1866

*"Are there no opportunities, no possibilities
at all, to avoid this war?"*

When Ludwig II ascended to the throne, Prussia and Austria, the two dominant powers on the European continent, were at war with Denmark to reclaim the German duchies Schleswig and Holstein. On June 7, 1866, Prussia illegally occupied Holstein, which was at the time under Austrian domination. Four days later, the Habsburg emperor demanded that the remaining states of the German Federation condemn this breach of contract. Thirteen of the states remained loyal to the Federation and the principle of law—including Austria itself, Hanover, Saxony, Württemberg, Baden, Hesse-Darmstadt, the Electorate of Hesse, and Bavaria—and now took to the battlefield against the eighteen smaller, north German states who depended on Prussia. During these crucial days the king remained at Berg Castle rather than returning to his residence in Munich, a choice that met with general indignation. Earlier, in February, the king had reacted with dismay when his secretary of foreign affairs, Baron von der Pfordten, had informed him about the impending threat of war.

Otto von Bismarck, prime minister and leading political figure in Prussia, concluded that the twenty-year-old king had a clearer perception of the political situation than his minister, for Ludwig felt no particular sympathy for Austria's

In the so-called **German War** of 1866, the Prussian army defeated the Austrians and their southern German allies at Königgrätz. In order to forestall French interference, Bismarck implored King Wilhelm I not to use his victory to military advantage. Instead, Bismarck employed the fact that

France demanded territory in southern Germany as an opportunity to align the South German states with him and to lead them to join a "Protection Agreement" with Prussia.

struggle for hegemony among the German states, and would have preferred to remain neutral. However, von der Pfordten, Ludwig's "angel of bad fortune", together with his supporters who were hostile to Prussia and the Protestants, forced the king to enter the German War of 1866.

On the eve of the confrontations, the king made clear that he was opposed to the war and argued for armed neutrality. But he did not wish to be accused of a "breach of word and faith," and therefore fulfilled his obligations to Austria and the German Federation. Ludwig's father, Maximilian II Joseph, had hardly concerned himself with building a strong Bavarian army; it was therefore "in no proper condition" for the war and could not be expected to reap laurels, in spite of the good morale of the troops and the "inborn pugnacity of the Bavarians."

On July 3, 1866, Prussia won the decisive battle of the war between Austria and Prussia at Königgrätz in the present-day Czech Republic, and on August 2 demanded a cease-fire from the state of Bavaria. When the queen mother wanted to convey her congratulations to the king, however, Ludwig was nowhere to be found.

After the cease-fire, a veritable storm of indignation against the military leadership of the land broke out across Bavaria. When the King was handed Bismarck's harsh and exaggerated peace conditions in August 1866, he took immediate and unexpected political initiative. The initial treaty demanded that Bavaria give up two districts in Lower Franconia, pay the considerable sum of 30 million guilders in reparations, enter a protective defensive alliance with Prussia, and—in case of war—place the Bavarian army under Prussian command. These demands deeply offended the king's understanding of sovereignty. During the peace nego-

---

The creation of a unified **German Empire** was the central idea behind Bismarck's Germany policy and was also at the core of the German War of 1866. His policy was eventually successful in 1871 when several factors flowed together. On the one hand, economic development began sooner or later to press toward a unified market; on the other hand, the emergence of a national awareness, which had been supported by democratic-liberal forces since the revolution of 1848, moved toward the same goal. Otto von Bismarck, prime minister of Prussia since 1862, knew how to unite these diverging forces for his unification

34   Battle of Königgrätz. Painting by Christian Sell, 1866.

tiations, he therefore requested his mother to use her influence with her cousin, King William I of Prussia, on behalf of Bavaria.

The queen mother came to her son's help and requested that the territorial as well as financial conditions be reduced. The response was all but flattering. William assured his cousin that he had already treated Bavaria with such consideration that his own people and troops were quite offended. In addition, as he related to the two Bavarian negotiators, "If Bavaria had remained neutral, as it had appeared to be up until the last weeks before the war, all of Germany would have followed suit. ... But once Bavaria sent up a war signal to the rest of Germany by making military preparations aimed against us, war became unavoidable—and in fact,

policy. From the outset, he was convinced of Prussia's leadership role. He expanded the military, which had a strong influence even on civil life in Prussia. Through alliances and even at times risky wars with changing partners, he managed to unite even the various parties of the Prussian Provincial Parliament and win their support for the idea of a German Empire under Prussian dominance, which he finally proclaimed after Napoleon III's defeat in 1871.

35   Park at Kissingen resort, August 12, 1866. Lithograph by C. Schweitzer.

civil war! ... Now, we hope to become friendly allies and only fight in unison against a mutual external enemy."

Compared to Bismarck's initial financial and territorial demands, it turned out that the stipulations of Ludwig's Prussian cousin were modest, indeed. The king wrote to his mother, "Fortunately, the conditions are better than could have been expected."

And yet, the country suffered the consequences of war, including a considerable number of ill and wounded troops returning from the field. Both the queen mother and the king exhibited compassion toward the suffering. Marie pointed out to her son how much joy a royal visit brought to the soldiers in the hospitals and that his photograph hung over

In the **German Customs Union**, the German states tried to create a single economic unit within German territory. Plans for such a union had existed since 1815, but it was not until 1828 that respective agreements were negotiated between Prussia and Hesse-Darmstadt, Bavaria and Württemberg (Southern German Customs Union). In 1833, both parties of the Southern German Customs Union aligned with the Electorate of Hesse, Saxony and Thuringia to form the German Customs Union. The Northern German states followed. By abolishing customs between states, the union was instrumental in unifying the German Empire.

every bed. In the wake of the civil war, Ludwig II established and funded the "Bavarian Society in Support of Invalids."

In July 1867, Bavaria entered into a closer relationship with the northern German states by joining the newly established German Customs Union, which aimed at the creation of a directly elected customs parliament. During the elections to the Zollverein in 1868 and the ensuing elections to the regional parliaments in 1869, significant political changes became evident. The majority of the Bavarian citizens now voted for the Catholic-conservative candidate rather than the liberal. Bavarian Foreign Minister Hohenlohe resigned and was succeeded by Otto, Count von Bray-Steinburg. These ministerial changes foreshadowed the French-Prussian conflict regarding the anticipated Spanish succession to the throne of Catholic Hohenzollern-Sigmaringen, a conflict which was finally settled by the Franco-Prussian War of 1870.

The Franco-Prussian War of 1870/71 and the foundation of the German Empire

> *"Count Bismarck wants to transform my kingdom into a Prussian province."*

The year 1866 must be considered an epochal one in German history, because the German Empire, founded in 1871, was "rather the result of the battle of Königgrätz [in the German War, 1866] than of the battle of Sedan," which was fought during the Franco-Prussian or French-German war.

Provoked by Bismarck's policies, France declared war on Prussia on July 19, 1870. The 1866 Mutual Protection Agree-

---

One of the reasons for the **French-German War** was the French hegemonic policy of Napoleon III, who tried to revise the territorial regulations of the Congress of Vienna (1815) to France's advantage. He fought wars, tried to purchase Luxembourg from the Netherlands, etc. Another reason was the justified fear of Prussia's efforts at hegemony among the German states. Bismarck's consciously shortened report of the protocol of a conversation between William I and a French diplomat regarding the abdication of Prince Leopold of Sigmaringen in Bad Ems (the so-called Ems-telegram) triggered the declaration of war.

ment between Prussia and Bavaria obligated Ludwig II to enter the war on the Prussian side. Ludwig telegraphed the king of Prussia: "My troops will fight with enthusiasm alongside your glorious allies for the justice and honor of Germany. May it be beneficial for Germany and for Bavaria." On July 16, Ludwig had ordered the mobilization of 55,000 soldiers, who were to be integrated into the Third Prussian Army. Coming from Berlin, the Prussian Crown Prince Frederick William arrived in Munich on July 27 and took over command of these troops. It must have been extremely difficult for Ludwig to receive him as commander of his troops in a friendly manner, for he was painfully aware that the consequences of the military alliance for Bavaria could not be foreseen.

Notwithstanding, he gave the Prussian crown prince a warm reception; a festive family dinner with music was arranged at the royal quarters of the palace. In the evening, they attended a performance of Friedrich Schiller's play *Wallenstein* at the Court Theater together. With an audience of 200 people, the theater was completely filled. When the two princes entered the royal box, they were enthusiastically greeted by the audience despite resentments about the recent defeat that had not yet been laid to rest. Still, national enthusiasm was stronger.

Late that night, the king wrote the Prussian crown prince a letter expressing his hope that King William I would appreciate and honor Bavarian loyalty, at the same time stating his expectation that Bavaria "would remain an independent state" after the war. The letter was handed to Frederick William on the following day as he was getting into the coach which was to travel with Prince Leopold and Ludwig's brother, Otto, to the front.

When the two fairytale princes embraced each other, the tall Nordic prince with blond mustache and brilliant eyes, and the dark-haired king of Bavaria who towered over the other by a full head, the audience cheered again and again so that I could not speak for minutes.

Theater director Ernst von Possart about Ludwig II
and the Prussian Crown Prince Frederick William
in the Royal box, July 27, 1870

The war itself bored the king. Nothing could motivate him to visit his troops. Instead, he stayed at Berg Castle, Hohenschwangau or Linderhof, enjoying the fresh air of the Bavarian Alps. Sitting in the bay window of his work room at Hohenschwangau, he commented in his diary on the incomparable view of sea and mountains, "I am attracted to the cold waters of the Alpine lake," and to Sybille Meilhaus, "I strongly long for a swift and lasting peace that will benefit Germany, but particularly my beloved Bavaria."

Shortly before the war the queen mother had already appealed to the women of Bavaria to be available for work that the Society for Women would soon demand of them. When war was declared, the central committee and district groups went straight to work raising funds, collecting clothes, and

36   A Bavarian calvary unit saving a Prussian hussar from French pursuit during the battle at Stürzelbronn on August 1, 1870. Painting by Louis Braun.

obtaining dressing materials and medications. Their responsibilities included the equipping of medical transports and the organization of emergency medical care for the hospital trains and the medical corps. The queen mother provided space for these efforts in the Royal Odeon. The enormous concert hall resembled a storage facility and very busy workshop.

At Fürstenried Castle and in its "Paradise Garden" Marie established military hospitals which she financed herself. Another hospital run by the Women's Society in Haidhausen was sponsored by Princess Alexandra. Here, both the queen mother and the king, as well as other members of the royal family, visited the invalid soldiers. The king, too, financed 240 beds for the wounded. His mother spent much of her time personally caring for the wounded.

The news of the surrender of MacMahon's French army and the capture of Napoleon III after the battle of Sedan on September 1, 1870, set off joyous celebrations all across Germany. On September 3, a festive procession of more than 5,000 participants took place in Munich. But the king, who was to be honored, did not attend—a disregard that was registered with great indignation. The curtains were drawn shut inside the windows of his private rooms in the residence. Showing her usual concern for her son's position, Marie assumed his obligation and appeared alone at a window in the residence where she was enthusiastically cheered by the passing crowds.

With the entry of the German troops into Versailles, Bismarck, the "Iron Chancellor," was close to achieving his goal of bringing about a German empire. The decisive negotiations on the unification of Germany began on October 20 in Versailles. Bavaria was represented by the minister of state, Count Gray; the minister of justice, Baron von Lutz; and the

37   The queen mother visiting wounded soldiers in a military hospital in 1866. Three years later, she and Ludwig II founded the Bavarian Women's Society of the Red Cross. Contemporary engraving.

38   The so-called "Letter to the Emperor."   ▶

minister of defense, Baron von Pranckh. Since Ludwig II had refused to leave his country, his brother Otto traveled to France to represent him; Prince Luitpold, later prince regent, was also present.

Prince Otto, who had briefly been with the Bavarian troops in France, had shown so little resistance to the strains of war that he was called back to Bavaria. The prince had already begun to show signs of mental disorder. He appeared miserable, as if he suffered from high fever, and his Prussian cousin was not at all sure whether Otto was able to comprehend his military and diplomatic instructions. Otto therefore returned to his brother who—not for the first time—had been considering resigning from the throne in Otto's favor. Upon seeing his brother face to face, however, Ludwig recognized his disastrous mental condition immediately.

Only a few days after Otto's return Maximilian, Count Holnstein, arrived at Hohenschwangau to deliver a written request by Bismarck asking the king of Bavaria to bid his Prussian cousin William I to accept the crown as emperor of Germany. At the time, Ludwig II was in bed with a toothache that he attempted to subdue with morphine and refused to receive Holnstein. Finally, Holnstein was admitted into the Tasso Room, the king's bedroom, where he copied Bismarck's letter under Ludwig's guidance, including a few changes:

"Most esteemed and powerful Grand Duke! Dearest brother and cousin!
Once the southern German states have joined the German Constitutional Treaty, presidential power over all German states will rest with Your Majesty. ... I have therefore ad-

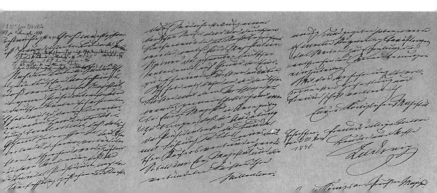

dressed the German princes to join with me in moving Your Majesty to unite the office of the president of the Confederation with the title of German Emperor. As soon as your Majesty and the allied princes have replied, I will authorize my government to do everything possible to support the appropriate agreements.

Assuring you of my complete respect and friendship
I remain
Your Royal Majesty's
Friendly cousin, brother, and nephew
Ludwig.

Hohenschwangau, November 30, 1870."

Count Holnstein rushed the precious document to Versailles where it was delivered to Bismarck by Prince Luitpold. On January 18, 1871, King William I of Prussia was proclaimed emperor of Germany in the Hall of Mirrors at Versailles— without the presence of King Ludwig II, even though the Prussian delegate in Munich had recommended to Bismarck in a telegram on November 17 to send the king six million guilders to cover his private building debts in order to induce the Bavarian monarch to travel to Versailles and attend the proclamation ceremony.

Otto, who had vehemently opposed Bismarck's policy from the beginning, attended the ceremony on his brother's behalf and wrote to him, "Oh Ludwig, I cannot even describe how very pained I felt during that ceremony, how every fiber in my body was opposed and outraged against everything that I saw. It all was so cold, arrogant, boastful, a sumptuous and magnificent show, heartless and empty. I felt suffocated and nauseated in that hall; only outside in the fresh air of the beautiful park could I breathe again." In November of 1870

39   Advent of the victorious   ▶
Bavarian troops in Munich. Painting
by L. L. Behringer, 1887.

Ludwig had already explained his position on the "emperor's letter" to his brother: "If Bavaria could be independent and remain outside the German Constitutional Treaty all this would be inconsequential; but politically this would be virtually impossible, since the people and the army would oppose this and the crown would lose all support in the country. Thus, horrible as it is, it is an act of political prudence, even necessity, and it is in the interest of the crown and the country that the king of Bavaria takes up this position."

Ludwig II certainly realized the consequences of Bavaria's integration into the German national state under Prussian leadership for the independence of his country. Through tenacious negotiations his delegates were able to secure a number of territorial and special rights, among them the right to maintain independent embassies abroad; to retain military autonomy in times of peace; the right of Bavarian residence; independent administration of the railroad, post, and telegraph systems; insurance of real estate, alcohol and beer taxation, as well as independent laws concerning all aspects of marriage. In connection with the founding of the empire Ludwig II later commented, "Since the ratification of these unfortunate agreements, I rarely enjoy a serene hour; I am sad and out of sorts."

On May 10, 1871, the peace treaty with France was concluded in Frankfurt, and on July 16, the victorious Bavarian troops returned to Munich. A week earlier Ludwig had written his brother, "Imagine, Otto, for political reasons and pressured from all sides, I have been forced to invite the crown prince [of Prussia] to the ceremony, a decision that almost drives me to despair; is it surprising that since the outbreak of all these events (war, signing of the agreement, etc.), ruling and the responsibility for people have become a hated obligation? Nevertheless, the royal position and its obligations are the most wonderful, the most valuable things on earth. I feel doomed that I was born into a time which turns all this to a burden."

Thus, on July 16, Ludwig II and his little-loved cousin Wilhelm rode to a review field near Nymphenburg where the Prussian crown prince accepted the salute of the Bavarian troops and awarded those who had earned particular merit the Iron Cross in the emperor's name. After the ceremony, there was a victory march led by William through Ludwigstrasse past the cheering crowds to Odeon Plaza where Ludwig II, who had returned alone to the city, awaited them with the queen mother and other members of the royal family. At night, the celebrations concluded with a festive performance of Paul Heyse's play *Peace* at the Court and National Theater. Ernst von Possart, an actor at the Bavarian court theater, had written and now presented the festive

Ludwig and Frederick William! Victorious pair,
The hope of young Germany! Hail to you always!
When God, our Lord, in order to bear witness to a nation
Creates such unbelievable perfection
That the century bows in honor
Before such a slight touch of his creative force,
Then the human being looks up in reverent silence
To the highest power of the world;
Whether desired happiness can be truly achieved,
whether it remains just a dream that tantalizes?
Through the weaving of fate he sees
What future generations will gain.

Let us welcome these festive hours,
Which we owe to the noble generosity

prologue in honor of the return of the victorious Bavarian troops.

On the following day, a family dinner was held on Rose Island in Lake Starnberg that ended with discord between the two cousins. Ludwig had offered the crown prince the command over the Bavarian Ulan Regiment, but William did not want to commit himself before he consulted with his father, the emperor. He also had doubts that his heavy body would fit into the narrow uniform of the Ulan regiment. The affront hurt Ludwig's feelings profoundly and he refused to attend the great military banquet that evening at the Glass Palace, to which 900 people had been invited. This absence, in turn, caused great indignation among many family members and guests.

What effect did the founding of the German Empire under Prussian leadership in 1871 have on the relationship between the Bavarian king and his Prussian-born mother? In fact, there were great difficulties, which are clearly evident in the king's letter of March 26, 1871, to the lady-in-waiting Therese, Baroness von Gasser. Ludwig had a hard time accepting the sacrifice of Bavarian interests. "As you may imagine, it is very painful for me to communicate with my mother, who is Prussia-German minded; our relationship is less harmonious than ever." He named his mother a "Prussian princess" and did not wish even to see her.

However, Ludwig II, who was destined to become the personification of a Bavarian king, was half Prussian himself. When the German emperor announced a visit to Bavaria in 1871 on his way to restore his health at the resort town of Bad Gastein, his nephew met him in Schwandorf; accompanied by cheering masses they continued to the festively decorated city of Regensburg and had dinner at the ancient

Of the German empire's darlings,
This festival's highest gain.
Yes, you are our precious possessions! Trustfully,
We lay our young fortune in your hand!
Hail to your friendship! With ardent grace
You crown the new, unified fatherland!
   *Ernst von Possart, "Festive prologue on the occasion of the victory celebration
after the battle of Königgrätz," July 16, 1871*

40   Ludwig II of Bavaria. Painting by August Spiess.

imperial Inn of the Golden Cross. Late that night, Ludwig returned to Berg Castle. When the emperor returned, Ludwig II had his uncle, Prince Luitpold, meet him in Rosenheim and accompany him to Munich. And then the queen mother dared to invite her Prussian relative to Hohenschwangau without asking the king's permission. As could be expected, Ludwig II was extremely irritable during the dinner. He hardly spoke to the emperor, but rather pursued a discussion about mental disorders with his mother's highest lady-in-waiting.

The king had never held back his resentment for the "hero emperor". He contemptuously referred to the Prussian rulers as "those robber Hohenzollern bandits, this Prussian trash," and discredited their bloodthirsty imperial policy as a "deep sin, even as a crime."

On the other hand, the money that flowed from Prussia into Ludwig's private accounts was most welcome. Since 1871, the king had received yearly 300,000 marks from "secret funds of the guelphs [the historical opposition of the German

I was under the impression that his thoughts wandered at the banquet and that he remembered only occasionally to come back to a conversation which did not surpass the ordinary courtly small talk. Nevertheless, I discovered in what he said a talented vivaciousness and a mind that was filled with a sense of future. During the pauses of the conversation he looked beyond his mother across the table to the ceiling and emptied a glass of champagne once in while and too hastily ...; despite this behavior, I felt that although he was bored by the occasion he nonetheless pursued his own independent thoughts, aided by the champagne. He made a sympathetic impression on me, although I have to admit with slight disappointment that my attempt to involve him in an interesting conversation remained unsuccessful. It was the only time that I met the young king personally, but I remained on positive terms with him as

emperors];" in 1884, a year of extreme need, he even received one million marks to cover his increasing construction debts.

Personal meeting with Bismarck

Bismarck and Ludwig II met each other only once in person. On August 16 and 17, 1863, the forty-eight-year old Bismarck, at the time Prussian prime minister and foreign minister, stayed in Munich and received an invitation to Nymphenburg castle for dinner. Bismarck was seated next to the Crown Prince Ludwig, then almost eighteen years old, while the queen sat across from him.

At the time, Ludwig apparently did not dare to face Otto von Bismarck. The Prussian prime minister's wife held that the young man imagined her husband to be "Siegfried" and feared that this would not hold true in a personal meeting. But perhaps Ludwig feared the opposite—that meeting this "Siegfried" face to face would make him seem even more powerful than he already was from afar. Instead of speaking, Ludwig corresponded with Bismarck, to whom he offered his royal equipage while he was on a cure in Bad Kissingen, in writing. When in summer 1874 an assassina-

41   Otto von Bismarck. Detail from the painting "War council in Versailles" by Anton von Werner, 1900.

soon as he ascended to the throne (March 10, 1864) until the end of his life. We corresponded regularly and I always had the impression of a businesslike clear regent with a national-German conviction, although with a predominant concern to preserve the federal principle of the imperial constitution and the constitutional privileges of his country.

Otto von Bismarck in
"Reflections and Memoirs"
about Ludwig II

tion attempt was made against Bismarck, from which he escaped almost unharmed, Ludwig II condemned the "abominable crime for whose failure I will thank God for ever." Bismarck, however, never accepted the king's invitation to the Bavarian Alps.

Ludwig II and Richard Wagner—
A Royal Friendship

"Oh King! Precious patron of my life!"

On March 23, 1864, the poet and composer Richard Wagner left Vienna hastily—financially and morally devastated, a fugitive on his way to Switzerland. When he passed through Munich on Good Friday, March 25, he noticed a photograph of the eighteen-year-old King Ludwig II in a store window and it occurred to him that such a patron would be his salvation. He continued on to Zurich, and then traveled to Stuttgart, where friends literally hid him from his creditors.

On May 3, 1864, the "miracle" occurred. The king's advisor, Franz Seraph von Pfistermeister, a trusted cabinet secretary for many years, delivered to Wagner a message from the king stating that he would "remove the master from every misfortune of fate." Delighted and grateful to be relieved of his financial problems so unexpectedly, Wagner replied, "I send you tears of divine emotion—poetry has come into my impoverished life that was yearning for love!—From now on my life, its ultimate poetry and music, belong to you, my gracious young king. Dispose of it as you wish!"

Wagner's message on the year of the king's birth also expressed the composer's deep gratitude: "The year in which *Tannhäuser* premiered … in the month of August, during which I felt so extraordinarily creative that I conceptualized both *Lohengrin* and *Mastersingers* at the same time, a mother gave birth to my guardian angel."

When Wagner and the monarch eventually met for the first time in the late afternoon of May 4 in the royal residence

---

Richard Wagner was in such a desolate state of mind at the time that he began to ponder his inglorious end and worked on his epitaph:
Here lies Wagner, who became nothing,
not even a knight of the most wretched order,
he cannot even lure a dog from behind the stove,
from universities not even a doctorate.

'Epitaphium,'
Munich, March 25, 1864

in Munich, the composer was strongly struck by Ludwig's appearance. The same day, he wrote to Eliza Wille, a close friend on the Mariafeld estate near Zurich, "He is unfortunately so very handsome and spirited, so sensitive and beautiful, that I fear his life will vanish swiftly, a fleeting divine dream in this harsh reality. ... My fortune is so immense that it quite shatters me."

Ludwig confronted the admired composer with very specific wishes. He demanded the completion of the *Nibelungen* cycle of operas, promising to finance the performances and all associated costs. What more could Wagner have desired? Ludwig summed up his impressions of their first meeting to his cousin, Princess Sophie of Bavaria, as follows: "I felt as

though we had exchanged roles." The king, who was much taller than the composer, had bent down to Wagner, and drawn him toward his heart, although he himself had received an oath of eternal loyalty.

The king provided Richard Wagner accommodation in a country house in Kempfenhausen on Lake Starnberg, near Berg Castle. When Wagner felt lonely out there, his future wife, Cosima von Bülow, the daughter of Franz Liszt and at the time married to the conductor Hans von Bülow, joined him with her

42   Richard Wagner. Painting by Franz von Lenbach (detail), 1870.
Wilhelm Richard Wagner, born on May 22, 1813, in Leipzig, grew up in Dresden. He started attending the Kreuzschule in 1822 under his stepfather's name, Geyer. He received his first lessons in composition from the first violinist of the Gewand-

hausorchester, Christian Gottlieb Müller, and studied counterpoint with the music director of the Thomas Church, Theodor Weinling. In 1833, Wagner was employed as a coach in Würzburg, where he became engaged to the actress Minna Planer. From 1837 to 1839, he served as the music director at the

two daughters, the three-and-a-half-year-old Daniela and the fifteen-month-old Blandine. In the weeks following, a clandestine affair developed between Wagner and Cosima von Bülow, of which neither Cosima's husband nor the king were aware for quite some time. On July 7, Hans von Bülow arrived in Munich—through Wagner's recommendation employed by the king as a soloist—and moved with his family into a house on Luitpoldstrasse. On October 15, 1864, Wagner moved into accommodations on Brienner Strasse 21, which the king had provided. Cosima, who managed Wagner's expansive correspondence, received her own office.

Ludwig's interest in Wagner's music had developed quite early. Already at the age of twelve, he had accidentally come across Wagner's treatises *The Work of Art of the Future* and *The Music of the Future* in the library of his great uncle, Duke Max in Bavaria. The "prose of a philosopher that rises up like a hymnal" would most certainly have been quite difficult reading for the boy. Although he did not comprehend their full meaning at the time, the ideas had begun to fascinate his imagination.

Ludwig's father, Maximilian II Joseph, who was the same age as Wagner, did not allow his son to attend the premiere of Wagner's opera *Lohengrin* on February 28, 1858. He considered it more important for the crown prince to become familiar with the Christian ruler's ethos of kingship through the grace of God, a principle which Ludwig's tutor Franz Steininger tried to exemplify by way of literature. For the sake of the properly virtuous ideal, they studied Friedrich Schiller's dramas, which Ludwig treasured throughout his life. Even some of Wagner's operas were suited for this purpose because they glorified the ideals of Christian virtues—for instance, the idea of sacrificial love—which Wagner per-

---

Riga Opera House. When his debts began to mount, he fled Riga with Minna Planer, now his wife, and went via London to Paris. Here, he met Heinrich Heine, Franz Liszt, and Hector Berlioz and began to study Beethoven's music. In 1843, he returned to Saxony and worked as a music director in Dresden.

Having actively participated in the revolutionary movement of 1848 and the May rebellion in Dresden in 1849, he was "wanted" and again fled to Switzerland. After a general amnesty in 1862, he moved to Vienna, where he divorced his wife. In 1864, again chased by creditors, he fled to Stuttgart.

sonified in the character of Elisabeth of Thuringia in his early opera *Tannhäuser*.

In August 1859 another of Ludwig's teachers, Theodor, the Count de la Rosée, gave him Wagner's essay *Opera and Drama*, which greatly inspired the boy's imagination. Finally, on February 2, 1861, his long-cherished wish came true. Accompanied by his beloved governess, Sybille von Meilhaus, the crown prince was allowed to attend the opera *Lohengrin*, conducted by Franz Lachner at the Court Theater in Munich. Nine years later, Ludwig confided to Wagner, "Although the performance was not brilliant, I understood the essence of that divine work. At the performance the seed of our love and life-long friendship was laid and the spark of our sacred ideals developed into a powerful flame." Deeply moved by the performance, the crown prince shed "tears of enchantment" and from that point on, started to memorize parts of

the libretto of *Lohengrin* and other Wagner operas.

Entries in the diary of the eighteen-year-old boy dating from June and August 1863 indicate that his teacher Franz Steininger gave him the librettos of the *Ring of the Nibelungen* and *The Mastersingers of Nuremberg* to read. On January 1 and 3, 1864, Ludwig noted in his diary: "After lunch concept of letter to Richard Wagner ... discussed my letter to Richard Wagner with Professor Stei-

43   Crown Prince Ludwig in 1861, the year of his first opera visit. Photograph by Hermann Holz.

niger yesterday." But even earlier, on May 26, 1862—that is, one year after first seeing *Lohengrin*, the sixteen-year-old crown prince had expressed his enthusiasm for the ingenious poet and composer in a letter to his cousin, Prince Heinrich of Hesse and on Rhine: "You ask if I like Wagner's music? I adore it. You want to know if I enjoy attending balls? I find them all right." On March 30, 1867, still only at the age of 21, the king again wrote to Wagner about his early love for the composer's work: "The first spark of sacred enchantment for your music was kindled in my soul by divine forces at a very young age; I am burning with excitement for your work."

The composer planned a special surprise for the king's nineteenth birthday on August 25, 1864. He arranged a "morning music" at Hohenschwangau Castle with excerpts from *Lohengrin* and *Tannhäuser*, and most importantly, composed for the occasion, his magnificent "March of Allegiance," which was dedicated to the king. The night before, he and the Munich music director and diligent composer Peter Streck, together with 80 musicians, traveled through terrible weather to arrive in Füssen, where the performance of Wagner's music was supposed to awaken Ludwig on his birthday morning. Unfortunately, a purported indisposition of the queen mother, who was staying at Hohenschwangau, snuffed out his carefully orchestrated plan. The dedicatory march for the king was not performed until a few months later, on October 5, 1864, a cold and rainy autumn day, in the courtyard of the king's suite in the royal residence. The composition was played a second time during a concert in the festively lit Residence Theater, to which only a distinguished circle of forty of Wagner's greatest admirers had been invited. Wagner conducted the court orchestra himself.

In his numerous theoretical **Essays on Music**, Wagner treated almost every topic concerning the relationship between drama and music. In Switzerland, he wrote the essays *Art and the Revolution* and *The Work of Art of the Future* (both 1849) and *Opera and Drama* (1851), in which he further developed his ideas. Wagner argued that music and poetry cannot be seen as separate entities, but that they reach their highest perfection only when merged in a "total work of art." In this process, poetry is the "generating" force while music is the "birthing" principle.

Ludwig II dreamed of building a large festival house for Wagner in Munich. He engaged Gottfried Semper, one of the foremost architects and construction experts of his time, with the planning. The building was to be erected on the right bank of the Isar River, south of the present Angel of Peace Monument, with a magnificent, wide boulevard leading in a straight line directly to the Brienner Strasse. Wagner, who had delayed the project several times, finally lost interest altogether. The king's cabinet had also responded with great reserve, so that Ludwig finally dropped the plans with much regret.

On November 2, the king invited Wagner to spend the week of November 11 to 18, 1865, with him at Hohenschwangau Castle. "Oh, we have much to share with each other," the king wrote to Wagner in his letter.

On Sunday, November 12, Wagner arranged for ten oboists to perform the so-called "Morning call" from *Lohengrin* at the top of the castle's tower. He and the king spent "wonderful days" together, during which Wagner learned to appreciate the "gentlest and most caring young man the world has seen."

But soon after the spectacular premiere of *Tristan and Isolde* at the Residence Theater in Munich, the political controversy concerning Wagner began to intensify. Very unwisely, the king had passed on to his cabinet some of Wagner's political suggestions. The cabinet had already begun to regard the composer with greatest suspicion. More than any other person, he had complete access to the king. When, in the midst of the mounting controversies, Wagner demanded that the king dismiss his senior cabinet members, Pfistermeister and von der Pfordten, the government confronted the monarch with an ultimatum, forcing him to "choose between his love and

Two days prior to the premiere of **Tristan and Isolde**, a parody named *Triftanderl and Süßholde* opened at a small theater on the outskirts of Munich: "Drama without music, a contemporary parody on the opera of the future in three acts in which much happens, plus a prelude by Richard Wagner—Wagnermaster, playwright and music dramatist." The title character, Triftanderl, is a rafter (from triften = rafting) from Ammerland, and Süssholde is the daughter of a rich baker from the small southern German town Wolfratshausen.

adoration of your faithful subjects or your friendship with Richard Wagner."

Ludwig II yielded. On December 6, the Upper Counsel to the Court of Appeals, Lutz, a colleague of Pfistermeister, delivered to Wagner the king's order, bidding him to leave Munich for a few months. Furiously, Wagner held Pfistermeister responsible, terming him "the most hateful of intriguers." On the evening of the very same day, however, the king attended the theater. Very depressed, he explained to Wagner in a wordy letter that he had had to act under the severe pressure of his entire cabinet, which had threatened to resign.

Wagner left Munich in the early morning hours of December 10. His opponents triumphed and the magistrate of Munich even considered a torchlight procession. Ludwig com-

44   Sketch of the unrealized Wagnerian festival house designed by Gottfried Semper to be located on the bank of the Isar River.

plained to Cosima in a letter, "I cannot endure to be separated from him for long. ... I suffer terribly." Wagner spent his exile in a villa in the Swiss town of Tribschen on an idyllic peninsula near Lucerne, while the king covered the costs of the "exile."

The royal family had also met Wagner with suspicion "because of his contradictions, which seamlessly merged theoretical and practical revolutionary ideas with an intimate friendship to the king." However, the general fear that Wagner influenced Ludwig's political decisions was certainly overrated from the very beginning.

After his expulsion from Munich in December 1865, Wagner took advantage of every opportunity to express his anger about the political smear campaign against him in Munich, "where people still seem to assume that I don't take my exile seriously and am engaging in subversive activities for God knows what end—perhaps the abolition of the political system and religion of Bavaria, in order to simply conduct the government from a huge opera house?"

On January 28, 1866, the king lamented, "My only friend! Joy of my life! Most precious gift! All and everything! Savior who makes me blissfully happy! ... Oh that I had a million tongues to convince them! Is it truly not possible for great minds to live in peace and happiness, adored by fellow men and inspiring them? ... That is the will of fate!—The 'world'

45 Contemporary caricature hinting at Wagner's purportedly great influence on Ludwig II.

will vanish before the example that we set. Ours shall be eternal serenity.—Please do write soon, blessed friend! Blossoming for the only friend until my last breath is drawn, true to the beloved until death!"

Performances of works by Richard Wagner in Munich

If Ludwig II was able to make an extraordinary contribution to music history in that he facilitated the production of Wagner's opera *Tristan and Isolde*, which had been rejected by the Vienna Opera House as not suitable, even impossible to be performed. On June 10, 1865, Hans von Bülow conducted the premiere at the Court Opera in Munich in the presence of an exhilarated king.

In 1867, severe controversies arose between Wagner and the king during the rehearsals for the new production of *Lohengrin*. The king—infatuated and closely identifying with the mysterious Swan Knight—wanted to impose his own stylistic preferences on the production. Wagner rejected the suggestions, and insisted on changing this "marionette performance," as he termed it—but without success. The dress rehearsal on June 11, 1867, caused new misunderstandings. For the title role Wagner had engaged his old friend, the tenor Josef Tichatschek, whom he warmly embraced after the rehearsal. The king, however, had noted through his opera glass that this "Lohengrin," instead of being the young hero he expected, was in fact an old man, supporting himself on a staff in the middle of the raft. Ludwig, infuriated, left the theater without a word to Wagner sitting in the box next to his, and returned to Berg Castle. The next day, the king informed Wagner that the sixty-year-old "sad knight" could

Josephine Kaulbach offered an account of the public's opinion of the royal friendship:
"I tell you, what people say for and against Wagner is crazy. Rumors spread like a monster with a thousand heads; the Wagner cult is becoming abominable. The infatuated young king turns everything in his surroundings into Tristan and Isolde and showers Wagner with verses and prose expressing his love."

come and have his feet washed the following year at the annual ceremony, but that he did not want to see him on his stage again. Deeply offended, Wagner returned to Tribschen in Switzerland without taking leave from the king.

On June 21, 1868, the premiere of *The Mastersingers of Nuremberg*, conducted by Hans von Bülow, was launched with great success at the Court Theater in Munich and became an extraordinary homage to Wagner—ironically in the very city that had expelled him only two-and-a-half years earlier.

The theater was filled to the last seat. Before the opera started, Ludwig II invited Wagner into the royal box and seated him at his side. At the king's request Wagner alone accepted the standing ovations after the second and third acts in the royal box. The courtiers were infuriated over what they assumed to be Wagner's presumptuousness. However, the composer who had been denounced and exiled was now finally "rehabilitated in an inexpressible way" as the news-

papers noted on the next day. Ludwig II commented, "I have seen the eternal with my own eyes; and I feel as though I have seen the most sacred."

Against Wagner's will—because the king owned the rights to *The Ring of the Nibelungen*—Ludwig forced the premiere of *Rheingold* to be performed prematurely on September 22, 1869, also in Munich, defying Wagner's

---

46 Ludwig and Malvina Schnorr von Carolsfeld as Tristan and Isolde on the occasion of the premiere in Munich 1865. Ludwig Schnorr von Carolsfeld, born July 2, 1836, was one of the celebrated tenors of his time. He sang the title roles in several Wagner operas. At Wagner's special request, he and his wife, Malvina Schnorr von Carolsfeld, née Garrigues (1825–1904), sang the title parts in *Tristan and Isolde* at the premiere performance. Preparation of the production required 77 rehearsals, making it immensely expensive—confirming the assessment of the Vienna Opera House which had rejected the work

expressed wish to perform the *Ring* only in its entirety. The composer demonstrably refused to attend the performance. One year later, on June 26, 1870, the premiere of the *Valkyrie* followed. Once again, Ludwig had forced the production, but this time, Wagner had resigned himself to his fate. The *Nibelungen* cycle owed its existence to Ludwig II. Wagner was eternally grateful that someone like the king could be such an ardent fan of his music and actually desire to see and support the various parts of the *Ring* cycle. The composer never lost sight of the fact that, without Ludwig, neither he nor his music would have existed.

Ludwig's birthday visit to Tribschen

After Richard Wagner had left Munich, Ludwig's desire for the composer reached desperate proportions. On April 21, 1866, he wrote him in a letter, "I love no woman, nor my parents, my brother, or any relative, I love no one with tenderness and with my whole heart except you!" Since Wagner refused to come to Munich, Ludwig decided to surprise him in Tribschen on the composer's fifty-third birthday. Despite the imminent outbreak of the German War, the monarch traveled to Switzerland incognito and stayed in Wagner's villa for two days.

Trying to deceive those around him, the king attended Cabinet Secretary Lutz's lecture on the morning of May 22 at Berg Castle, and then, accompanied only by his valet Völkl, hurried secretly to Biessenhofen where he caught the express train to Lindau. From there he continued by steamship to Romanshorn on the Swiss side of the lake and on by train to Lucerne. In the late afternoon, he appeared in front of

as unproducible. The king kept his promise and absorbed the entire costs of the production. Ludwig Schnorr von Carolsfeld also sang the title role of *Lohengrin* at its premiere performance. He died prematurely on June 21, 1865, in Dresden.

Wagner's villa, dressed in a cape and a hat, and had himself announced as Walther von Stolzing.

Wagner, however, had been previously informed of the imminent "surprise" because several days earlier, the king had sent his beloved young adjunct Paul von Thurn und Taxis, his "Good Man Friday," to Tribschen. The messenger had been assigned the pseudonym "Melot," another character in the opera.

Private performances for the king

*"I want to be the observer myself,
not be observed by the crowd!"*

"From near and far thousands will come on a pilgrimage to the national festival"—these were Ludwig's words, referring to his plans for the Wagner festival house on the banks of the Isar River. The king himself, however, preferred private performances from which all other guests were excluded. He confided to the actor-producer Ernst von Possart, "As long as people keep staring at me and observing my facial expressions through their opera glasses, I cannot maintain the illusions of the theater. I want to be the observer, observe myself, not be observed by the crowd!"

After the performance of *Iphigenie* by the actress Clara Ziegler, Ludwig announced that from now on he would no longer show himself to the audience. On May 2, 1872, starting with the comedy *Countess du Barry*, based on *Ancelot* by L. Schneider, a series of 209 private performances were produced at the Residenz Theater and at the National Theater between 1872 and 1885—including 44 operas by Richard Wagner, Giuseppe Verdi, Christoph Willibald Gluck, Giacomo Meyerbeer, Daniel François Esprit Auber and others.

All performers who were engaged in these performances were strictly forbidden to speak about them. There exists only one authentic account, by the actress Charlotte Wolter of the Burgtheater in Vienna. As a guest artist, she had played Mme. Pompadour in a private production of *Narcissus* for the king on May 9, 1885. "The actors and actresses gathered on the stage at 11:30 P.M. There was absolute silence. Precisely at midnight, a bell rang. The king stepped into his box and the curtain rose." At this moment, Charlotte Wolter felt completely lost, wondering how she could act in front of an empty black box. "Eventually I stepped on the stage. I missed the contact with the audience. What kept me going was the realization that the invisible observer in the royal box loved the arts and that I knew, behind all his fantasies, there burns a genuine passion for my art. This thought flattered and calmed me at once. I knew that the king did not take his eyes off me, that he sat in his box entirely concentrated and attentive and so deeply immersed in what he saw that he even controlled his breathing because he did not want to give away his presence or distract himself. All this was new and strange to me. People

Ludwig's trip did not remain unnoticed in Munich and—occurring at a time of high political tension—caused general indignation. Although unfounded, again Wagner was made responsible and a new smear campaign was launched against him, Hans von Bülow and the "carrier pigeon Madame Hans" (Cosima von Bülow). Both the people and the parliament of

47   Tribschen on a sliver of land in lake Vierwaldstätter. Etching from the 19th century.

Munich received the king coldly when he returned from Switzerland; some even cursed and swore at him in the streets of the city.

Bayreuth

On May 22, 1872—Wagner's birthday—the foundation stone for the Festival House was laid in Bayreuth because Wagner had refused to return to Munich. The funds for the construction, which had been raised exclusively from private sources, began to run out, thus endangering the completion of theater. Once again, Wagner had to turn to the king to ask him to act as a guarantor for the Bayreuth project. With some hesitation—his own accounts were strained to the hilt—the king promised help and saved the project.

On April 28, 1874, the Wagner family moved into their private house, which still carries the inscription "Here, where my imagination (*Wähnen*) found peace (*Frieden*)—Wahnfried—

ridiculed him for his inclination to have plays performed exclusively for himself, but I must confess that I understand it completely. This way, the king excludes everything that could disturb him or the audience."

Around 4:00 A.M. when the last curtain had fallen, the performers had to remain motionless on the stage so that the king would not be disturbed. He had the habit of remaining seated for some time and pondering the experience, "quite like someone who has difficulties returning to reality."

be thy name." Before the villa stands Kaspar von Zumbusch's magnificent bust of Ludwig II. The king had contributed 25,000 thaler to the purchase of the site and the villa's construction.

In the summer of 1876, the first Bayreuth Festival opened with three performances of the entire *Ring of the Nibelungen*. The king attended all four dress rehearsals. He arrived in Bayreuth on the night of August 5 to 6, strictly incognito, accompanied only by the Head Stablemaster Count Holnstein and an adjutant. At 1:00 A.M., the royal train stopped on the open track near the Rollwenzel House. Wagner met Ludwig with a carriage and took him to Eremitage Palace, located about an hour from Bayreuth. During the festival, Bayreuth was aglitter with light, by day and especially by night. Wherever the king appeared he was welcomed with excitement. Around 8,000 people visited the festival in the first summer, 2,000 of them from abroad.

Two-and-a-half weeks later, from August 27 to 31, the king returned again to the Bayreuth Festival House to experience the performance of the third *Ring* cycle. He even wanted to command a fourth performance, but Wagner steadfastly refused.

After the performance of *The Valkyrie*, the king strolled through the park of the Eremitage Palace with Wagner, as some town officials and a few servants and sang arias of the *Ring* out loud. Before the performance of *Siegfried*, banker Friedrich Feustel, a member of the board, hailed the king, although Ludwig had strictly forbidden such ovations. At the end of *Götterdämmerung*, the king rose in his box and gave a standing ovation. Wagner, in turn, celebrated the king in a short address as his "collaborator." When Ludwig departed late that night, the citizens of Bayreuth lined both sides of the

48   The Bayreuth Festival House. ▶
Watercolor, 1876.

road, holding burning torches and glowing lanterns. As the king boarded the train, an orchestra played the Bavarian national anthem.

Despite its tremendous popular success, the first festival turned out to be a financial disaster. Deeply in debt himself because of his ambitious building projects, the king "was unable to make another financial sacrifice." Not until one-and-a-half years later, in March 1878, was the king able to support Wagner once more. Advised by the banker Friedrich Feustel, Cosima addressed the king, requesting him to grant Wagner royalties on his works for the Munich performances. On this basis, Ludwig was willing to grant a new loan of 100,000 marks plus interest which—like the first loan of 216,152 marks in 1874—was completely repaid by the Wagner family by 1906.

Ludwig contributed the services of the orchestra of the Court Theater, along with its conductor Hermann Levi, for the performance of *Parsifal* at the Bayreuth Festival of 1881. According to Wagner there was, however, a "dark" spot in Levi's life: he was Jewish. Wagner tried to convert him to Christianity, a suggestion which astounded the conductor.

Wagner was informed unequivocally that the orchestra would be provided only with its conductor. Eventually he backed down, and when he agreed to accept Levi (whose performance he later on highly praised) with high-sounding words written to the king, Ludwig countered, "I hope the artists from Munich whose participation you wish, will live up to their reputation! That you, beloved friend, make no distinction between Christians and Jews during the performance of your great and sacred work deserves my admiration. Indeed, nothing is more disgusting and unproductive than such controversies. In essence, all men are brothers despite confessional differences. October 11, 1881."

Wagner's last opera, *Parsifal*—the king's favorite work— premiered on July 26, 1883. Although Wagner had sent a special invitation and greatly desired his presence, Ludwig declined with the excuse that, if he accepted, he would be obliged to receive the attending foreign representatives. Thus, the faithful royal supporter of Wagner saw *Parsifal* only after the composer's death.

The last meeting

In Munich, the king met Wagner for the last time at the end of autumn, 1880. On December 31, 1879, the Wagner family decided to travel from Bayreuth to Italy. They took a specially reserved coach from Munich to Posilipo near Naples where they had rented the magnificent Villa Angri for six months. Wagner wrote to the king that the coach had used up more of his finances than he could afford. Ludwig understood immediately and granted him an "allowance" of 5,200 Italian lira "in order to prolong the stay which was so beneficial to the

Wagner expressed his **anti-semitism** in his essay *Jews in Music* in 1850, which was directed explicitly against Giacomo Meyerbeer, one of the most successful opera composers of his time. At the roots of Wagner's anti-Semitism lies an excessive preoccupation with Nordic and Germanic mythology, paired with perverted Christian dogma. These distinctive features of Wagner's œuvre fascinated the National Socialists.

master's health." The new secretary of the court, Ludwig von Bürkel, who was as sympathetic to Wagner as his monarch, assured Cosima "that there was no intention to pressure the master and his family to return to the cold German winter." After an eleven-month stay—Wagner's health had not improved—the entire family returned to Munich on October 30, 1880. To surprise Wagner, the king had arranged performances of the operas *The Flying Dutchman*, *Tristan and Isolde* and *Lohengrin*, in part because he wanted Cosima and the children to attend performances of these works. The "private" performance of *Lohengrin* on November 10, during which Wagner sat in the royal box next to the king, was to be their last direct meeting.

The following day, Wagner discussed the *Parsifal* production with the director Hermann Levi. The composer was very tired and not at his best. The orchestra rehearsals went extremely well, but Wagner was annoyed because the king came late. When Ludwig finally arrived and asked that the prelude be repeated, Wagner could not refuse. When the king also requested to hear the prelude to *Lohengrin*, the composer exploded. Focused on *Parsifal*, Wagner was unable to shift spontaneously to the earlier work. He left the rehearsal with Cosima and went back to the hotel. In spite of this angry last encounter, there was still a regular exchange of letters between Ludwig and the Wagner family, among them the aforementioned invitation of Ludwig to attend the premiere of *Parsifal* in 1883.

When **Wagner left Munich** in 1865, he again settled in Switzerland. Cosima von Bülow followed him, eventually divorcing her husband and marrying the composer in 1870. Hans von Bülow nonetheless continued to conduct the premiere performances of Wagner's operas. After 1870, Wagner again began writing theoretical essays, and even contacted Friedrich Nietzsche. On February 13, 1883, the composer died of heart failure during a trip to Venice.

**"Sublime King! Most gracious Lord" and "Most honored Friend!"—
Ludwig II and Cosima von Bülow in Munich**

Cosima, born on December 24, 1837, in Como, Italy, as the daughter of the
composer and pianist Franz Lizst and Countess Marie d'Angoult, was
only eight years older than Ludwig II. Nevertheless, she became his
maternal friend and adviser and served as an important mediator between Richard Wagner and his patron. Her marriage to the pianist,
conductor and Wagner-admirer Hans von Bülow in Berlin was not primarily based on great affection. It is therefore not surprising that Cosima
von Bülow and Richard Wagner became lovers after November 1863.
Beginning in November 1864, Cosima became Wagner's lover, house-
keeper, secretary and clever diplomat. On April 10, 1865, she gave birth to
Wagner's daughter, Isolde, while Hans von Bülow conducted the first
orchestra rehearsal of *Tristan and Isolde*.

It may have been a sign of particular respect that the king wrote Cosima von Bülow through his state secretary von Pfistermeister on May 20,
1865, from Berg Castle. The minister requested her to "please advise
what His Majesty could do to make Wagner happy on his upcoming
birthday." On that occasion, von Pfistermeister spoke about Cosima's
"enlightened, clear and calm mind as the best mirror for Wagner's ingenious thoughts."

On June 9, 1865, we find the following entry in Wagner's annals:
"Berg: Cos. Pfist. König," indicating that Cosima had been invited to Berg
Castle for the first time, together with Richard Wagner and Franz Seraph
von Pfistermeister. We find a similar entry on July 16, 1865, with the
addition that Cosima's two older children were also present.

On June 4, 1865, the king thanked Cosima, through Pfistermeister, for
the delivery of a collection of manuscripts and some older articles about
Wagner. Ludwig admired the diligence and consistency "with which you,
adored friend, have gathered the dispersed materials for the master like
a busy bee." Pfistermeister closed the letter to Cosima adding a small
anecdote, "which testifies to the very strange talent of our beloved
Majesty. When I returned from a long ride the other night—so he told
me—and took a warm bath, standing in the water in the big bathroom
I clapped my hands alternately and with differing force on the surface
of the water. The sequence of the sounds that resulted reminded me
immediately of the last motif of *Tristan*. Suddenly the entire scene—Isolde
bent over Tristan's corpse—with all musical detail appeared miraculously
in my ears. Isn't it strange?"

Although the king's letters to Wagner never failed to include greetings to Mrs. and Mr. von Bülow, Wagner mentioned Cosima himself for
the first time on June 25, 1865: "In the evening hours, I drove back from
Lake Tegern to Munich where I had left behind my brave lions [Mr. and
Mrs. Schnorr von Carolsfeld]. My wonderful, intimately trusted friend,
Franz Liszt's daughter, accompanied me. Her entire life follows a single
thread—and this is contained in the magic bond that connects you, my
most precious king, to me. During a private walk in the beautiful valley
on the previous day, I had shared with my friends some of the dis-
appointing experiences with people and life. My friend was still filled

with disgust about them. Then she fell into one of her ecstatic bouts of sleep, which befall her all of a sudden from time to time. During these, she speaks clearly and consistently about dream images, which she sees in the deepest slumber, but has no memory at all as soon as she awakes. Suddenly, she began as follows: 'Oh yes! This is exactly how I imagined the grail church. Yes, this is the appropriate image for the altar. Perhaps this is the deeper meaning of Michelangelo's "Last Judgment" in the Sistine Chapel. One side represents your works, one more brilliant than the other; the other side your life experiences, one more horrible than the other; and above all in the clouds—Parsifal (as you are called among us, treasured friend!) as world judge. And below, down below—oh, how awful! I don't want to look! Eternal treason!' She

49   Cosima von Bülow. Painting by Franz von Lenbach, 1870.

fell silent—and woke up." Wagner praised "friend Cosima" to the king also as the author of his autobiography, *My Life* (July 21/22). Apparently, as he dictated, she wrote down and edited the final copy, which was sent to the king in successive stages.

On August 20, 1865, shortly before the king's twentieth birthday, Wagner eventually mentioned his lover directly. "Be the guiding planet of the circle of a few chosen ones into whose loving care fate has entrusted me and my works. A noble, profound and trustworthy woman is intimately connected with this circle. If you want to know something about me that you do not understand, ask this rare being who—pure as the primary springs of the Norns [primordial figures in Nordic mythology]—will mirror everything to you. Turn to her, my noble, wonderful friend! I no longer belong to anyone in this whole world except you and these two [Cosima and her daughter Daniela]!"

After this confession, Cosima von Bülow and Ludwig II entered into a correspondence in which Cosima became the mediator between the king and the genius. On first impression, the king's letters appear unbelievably effusive. A systematic analysis, however, reveals that they contain hundreds of cryptic literary quotations, stretching from Dante through Goethe to librettos of Wagner's and Liszt's operas and oratorios. Ludwig also employed liturgical texts and verses from the Bible. In short, the letters prove that the young king was well-read and educated.

After Wagner was forced to leave Munich in 1865 and Cosima von Bülow joined him in Tribschen, the composer asked Ludwig to publish a statement, formulated by Wagner himself, in the form of a letter to Hans von Bülow, intended to silence the rumors of his inappropriate relationship with Cosima. The king granted his wish and consented to the publication of the letter. In the long term, however, the betrayal did not remain undetected. Responding to Court Secretary Düfflipp, the king wrote, "Is it possible that the sad rumor is true? Is it really a case of adultery? If so, they will be sorry!"

When Wagner and Cosima pressured Ludwig to withdraw the pension from Malvina Schnorr von Carolsfeld, then widowed, because she had confided to Ludwig the truth about their relationship, the king replied at the end of 1867, "I am utterly disgusted by the constant intrigues and complaints of Wagner, the Bülows and their dependents. I have been so very lenient and patient with these people, have granted them so many favors, that they have every reason to be content and grateful. The threads of my patience are finally starting to wear thin."

Cosima accomplished a psychological masterstroke, when she reacted to the king's intention to resign from the throne on July 24, 1866, by reminding Ludwig II that she had always believed in the principle of "kingship of God's grace" as in a religion. "Therefore, I believed solely in you, my noble king, that as the king, you must lift up the arts. I pray to God from whom the kings receive their power and dignity, that He may lift your heart and console you, that He will send you an angel as appeared to our Savior on the Mount of Olives, so that you who make others happy will also find happiness and peace. For ever true and loving, in deadly fear and sublime joy!"

He had written to her, "May I ask you to prepare the Beloved for my decision to step down from the throne. Oh, that he may be compassionate and not insist that I must bear this torture any longer. ... As the king, I cannot be one with him. I implore you, write to me soon, send me joyful news, assure me that the Unique and Adored understands that there are higher crowns and nobler empires than these unhappy ones on earth! Make him understand the passion of my love for him, oh friend; only then will I begin to live. Liberate me from this shadow existence!" (July 21, 1866).

The break-up with their patron, which Cosima had anticipated after her decision to stay with Wagner in Tribschen, did not occur. The confession of their love for each other and their love for the king brought relief to them all—a relief through love. Above all stand the king's words to Cosima of March 1869, "Forget all you suffered, forget it on my behalf, forgive me or else you punish me as well and I do not deserve it. Perhaps you do not realize how truly and intimately I love you. After the Friend, you are the most precious and admired being on earth."

Many years later, on April 29, 1878, Cosima noted in her diary: "When Richard recalls our old difficult times in Munich, 'How on earth did I bear it?'" But she also added that Richard Wagner truly acknowledged that "the king was the only person who had unflaggingly stood by their side during the years of separation from Bülow, the years of the 'illegitimate' relationship." The correspondence between Ludwig II and Cosima von Bülow is impressive truth of this.

A king mourns a genius

> *"The artist whom the entire world now mourns—*
> *I was the first to recognize and save him for the world."*

Richard Wagner's early and unexpected death on February 13, 1883, in Venice affected the monarch deeply. When he received the news he cried out "Terrible! Awful!" and asked to be left alone. On February 17, the special train with Cosima Wagner and the master's remains arrived in Munich. The king did not meet her at the train station. In his place, Count von Lerchenfeld presented her a palm wreath whose white-blue dedication read: "To the poet of word and music, to Master Richard Wagner, from King Ludwig II of Bavaria." An orchestra played Beethoven's funeral march and the funeral march from *Götterdämmerung*. Count Ludwig von Bürkel, who delivered the letter expressing the king's condolences to Cosima Wagner, was received by her daughter Daniela von Bülow.

In the summer of 1885, Cosima Wagner asked Ludwig to assume the sponsorship of the Bayreuth Festival 1886. The king replied in a note of September 21, 1885, "There is no doubt that the coming performances … will be an extraordinary success. … I will be delighted to accept your offer to

---

Letter of consolation from Ludwig II to Cosima Wagner after the unexpected death of the composer in Venice:

Most precious madam, dearest friend,

No words can express the deep pain that fills my soul at the profound and unfathomable loss that we have suffered. What a terrible stroke of fate has hit you and the poor children, all of us, the friends and numerous admirers of the great master and irreplaceable friend. He was the noblest of minds. Who would have thought that he would be taken from us so early! Be assured, precious beloved friend, that your eternally true friend shares with you and the dear children the bitter pain in the depth of his soul that the Beloved has passed away so terribly early. …

God bless you! He has made his peace, is no longer suffering! How much I love you for having sacrificed your strong love to the Unforgettable so unflaggingly, it is you … who brought true beauty and happiness to his life.

In cordial closeness, eternally your and your precious family's true friend Ludwig

Munich, February 16, 1883.

sponsor your noble and wonderful enterprise. ... Your true friend Ludwig."

In a rather ironic twist of fate, by the time that the curtain went up in the Bayreuth Festival House in July 1886, King Ludwig II had already passed away. What he had written to Wagner on August 4, 1865, came to be, namely, that "when we both no longer exist, our work will stand as a shining example for those who come after us. Our work will give pleasure to generations, and hearts will be enchanted by the divine and eternal arts."

50   "You both inhabit the heights of humanity!" Richard Wagner and Ludwig II at Berg Castle. Painting by Kurt Rozynski, 1890.

Operas by Richard Wagner
1833 *The Wedding* (Fragment)
1833 *The Fairies*
1836 *The Ban of Love or The Novice of Palermo*
1842 *Rienzi, the Last of the Tribunes*
1843 *The Flying Dutchman*
1845 *Tannhäuser and the Singing Competition on the Wartburg*
1850 *Lohengrin*
1865 *Tristan and Isolde*
1868 *The Mastersingers of Nuremberg*
1883 *Parsifal*
The Ring of the Nibelungen:
1869 *Rhinegold*
1870 *The Valkyrie*
1870 *Siegfried*
1876 *Twilight of the Gods*

Castles, Castles, Castles

"... my building projects ... the main source of joy in my life"

In the long history of the House of Wittelsbach, King Ludwig II was not only one of the most important patrons of the performing arts, but also one of the most prolific builders. His architecture gained its unmistakable character from its close connection with the theater—particularly with Richard Wagner's operas. Unlike his father and grandfather, both avid builders, whose architecture generally followed classicist ideals, Ludwig favored the neo-baroque and the neo-rococo styles. With Neuschwanstein, he turned to neo-romantic inspiration, and in addition showed a strong tendency toward oriental design.

The architectural works of Ludwig II are strongly imbued with his unique personality. He developed his own concepts, which might well include every detail of form and content, and transmitted his orders to the court secretary. In his role of both architect and master-builder, Ludwig tolerated no intervention from the skilled—but never important—painters, sculptors or poets in his employ.

The king handed out major commissions to the court furniture manufacturer Pössenbacher, the embroidery studios of Jörres and Wollenweber, the court metalworkers Köbel and Moradelli, the Zettler royal glass works, the Mayer Court Art Institution and many others. The continual artistic activity turned Munich into a European metropolis of the commercial arts that could favorably compare itself with Vienna or Paris—where the king also ordered artwork.

Castles, built or planned
Neuschwanstein
Linderhof
Herrenchiemsee ("Bavarian
Versailles", construction costs:
c. 20 million florins; inhabited by
Ludwig II for a single week)
Castle on the Falkenstein (planned,
but not built)

Ludwig built predominantly in poorer, rural areas. His building projects required construction of new roads, so-called princely highways, which provided work and bread for much of the rural population. The same effect had occurred under his father, Maximilian II Joseph, when large court entourages visited the king's "little lodges" for hunting or mountain climbing. On such occasions, a large number of people and animals needed quarters and provisions. Such activity always brought a certain level of economic development in its wake.

Ludwig's father had already established a hunting lodge in Graswang Valley near the Ettal monastery. Here Ludwig chose to build his extremely luxurious Linderhof Castle. The project was called "Meicost Ettal," an anagram for the French King Louis XIV's famous words *L'état c'est moi*—"I am the State."

Of his three new royal palaces, Linderhof is the only one whose completion Ludwig lived to see. During the last eight years of his life, he often spent long periods here. In homage to Louis XIV, called the Sun King, whom Ludwig greatly admired, the castle's interior design gleams with the spirit of the French late baroque and rococo. Louis' symbol, a sun with rays, as well as his motto, *Nec pluribus impar* ("No unequal match for many"), are repeatedly in evidence in the castle, is

also large, dominating equestrian statue of the French king. The castle's largest room is the impressive royal bedchamber, also clearly designed in the spirit of Versailles. Even today, the dining room remains one of the great attractions. The king's designs provided for a "magic" self-serving dining table (*Tischlein-deck-dich*), which rose into the dining hall fully set with food and drink so that Ludwig could enjoy his meal completely undisturbed by his servants. During these lonely meals, he could gaze at a pastel portrait of Madame Dubarry, done in 1872, which hung in the adjacent pink cabinet along-side portraits of Ludwig XV, Madame Pompadour and thir-teen members of the French nobility.

In this castle nestled in the Graswang Valley, the king as usual turned night into day. Normally he did not arise before 5 o'clock in the afternoon, breakfasted, and then strolled through the grounds to admire the park fountains. He would move on to the southern terrace to visit the larger-than-life-size bust of Queen Marie Antoinette, and next to the circular temple with its statue of Venus. Between 8:00 and 10:00 P.M., Ludwig heard the cabinet secretary's report and then had his dinner. He usually retired around 2:00 to 3:00 A.M.

Depending on his mood, Ludwig might also undertake nocturnal rides. At his disposal were the magnificent state coach built to his specifications in 1871 by the royal wagoner Franz Paul Gmelch in Munich, or a smaller coach, built by royal wagoner Johann Michael Mayer according to designs by court theater director Franz Seitz. The latter, drawn by six horses, was particularly suited for rides in the landscapes surrounding Linderhof and Neuschwanstein castles. Its orn-ate roof was decorated with a small sculptural group of genii and amoretti carrying the king's insignia. The four corners were decorated with small blue-and-white bouquets of heron

◄ 51 Castle and park of Linderhof Castle, seen from the circular temple across the southern terrace garden looking toward the main building.

and ostrich feathers. In the winter the small coach was easily transformed into a magnificent sleigh. The king also used a sleight of his own design—a two-seated gilded Renaissance sleigh decorated with putti. After 1885, the crown, which also functioned as a lantern, and some other lights were operated by electrical batteries, which were installed in the sled's box.

Inspired by Wagner's opera *Tannhäuser*, the Venus Grotto is found in a wild gorge northeast of the castle. Ludwig intended to replicate the Blue Grotto on the island of Capri in the Mediterranean. The structure consists of a nearly 33-foot-high (10 m) main grotto erected by landscape architect Carl von Effner and court architect Georg Dollmann and containing a painting of *Tannhäuser with Lady Venus* by August von Heckel. It is the largest artificial—but deceptively natural-looking—stalagtite cave in the world. The grotto could be entered the year around, and the water of the lake could not

52 Ludwig in his putti-decorated sleigh during one of his nocturnal excursions. Detail of a painting by R. Wenig.

53 View of the Venus Grotto ▶ near Linderhof, illuminated with blue light. Watercolor by Heinrich Breling.

only be heated, but also stirred by a wave machine when the king desired.

In 1877 the grotto was fitted with 24 colored electric arc lights, a pilot project by Werner von Siemens. A projector to create rainbows and an artificial waterfall that could be turned on at will rounded out the illusion. The king visited the grotto only at night. First he fed the swans that had been brought in from the park, then he and a servant stepped into the oak-and-linden boat decorated with gilded carvings. The cave was illuminated in Ludwig's favorite colors of red, pink, green and blue, which cast a magic shimmer on the waves, rocky walls, the swans and the roses. Thus the king glided through the grotto in the magnificent shell-shaped boat. However, anyone peeking behind the scenes discovered "a melancholy prose tale:" a very stressed electrician and seven boilermen to tend the water-heaters.

In late 1877, Ludwig had a Moorish Kiosk erected on Hennenkopf Hill behind Linderhof Castle. He had first seen the Kiosk at the International Exhibition in Paris in 1867, and bought it from its former owner, the Prussian banker and railroad magnate Bethel Henry Strousberg, after he went bankrupt. In the interior, the greatest attraction is still the peacock throne cast in enameled bronze that Ludwig had made from a design by Franz Seitz.

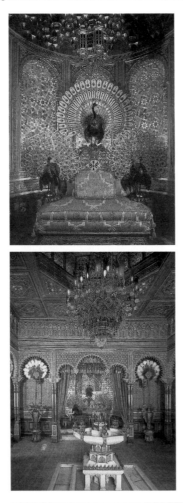

In 1876, the structure known as Hunding's Hut was built near the source of the Ammer River, in the midst of the forest at the foot of the Kreuzspitze. This lodge, intended to be an architectural reconstruction of the setting from the first act of *The Valkyrie*, consists of a hall with two siderooms built of "massive rough-hewn beams constructed around the trunk of an ancient, widely branched ash tree." Since the Linderhof forest yielded only beech wood, the order was changed to "double beech covered with heavy ash."

Old hunting weapons, animal skins, and hunting trophies completed the interior of Hunding's Hut—and in the trunk of the ash tree, Siegmund's sword 'Nothung' had been stuck. An artificial lake in front of the hut completed the romantic setting.

In his later years, the king gladly retreated to the lodge for extensive reading on a bearskin bed, or invited young

54, 55   Peacock throne (top) and interior of the Moorish Kiosk near Linderhof Castle.

men to "mead-drinking parties" in the ancient Germanic style. In 1871, he wrote to Richard Wagner, "I want to escape the hellish dusk that engulfs me and rather be happy in the divine dusk (*Twilight of the Gods*) of the tranquil mountain loneliness, far away from the 'day,' that hated enemy, far from the singing illusory brightness of the sun!"

Near Hunding's Hut, but modeled after the stage design of the third act of Wagner's opera *Parsifal*, Gurnemanz's Hermitage was constructed in 1877. The king especially enjoyed celebrating Good Friday here. In 1945, both Hunding's Hut and the Hermitage went up in flames. Not until 1990 was Hunding's Hut reconstructed in its original form at another location in the park surrounding Linderhof Castle.

One of the great attractions of the International Exhibition in Paris in 1878 was a Moroccan House that could be dismanteled into separate pieces. The king acquired it and had it erected near Hunding's Hut. Considerable alterations were made to both the exterior and interior in keeping with the king's lavish tastes, and the color scheme was changed with an abundant use of Ludwig's favored colors red, blue and gold. After the king's death, the house was sold to a man from Oberammergau.

According to Theodor Hierneis, Ludwig's cook, meals were adjusted to suit the places visited. In the Moroccan House, "pyramid" or violet punch was served alternately. The former had a pineapple taste and was drunk with date tarts. The violet punch, made of dried violet roots marinated in French champagne and exuding a strong odor, was served with petits fours adorned with candied violets. Violets would of course have been unsuited to the mood at Hunding's Hut, where Ludwig dined at a simple wooden table decked

56 Gurnemanz's Hermitage.

with deer horns full of mead, silver stags or deer filled with whipped cream for the mocha, and small silver owls as salt and pepper dispensers.

Ludwig's desire for "tranquil mountain loneliness" increased over the years. Although he had inherited 18 hunting lodges from his father, he built another royal lodge in 1870/71 on the Schachen mountain at a height of almost 6000 feet (1866 m). The exterior resembled an oversized Swiss chalet; in the interior, a spiraling staircase led to the upper floor, which opened into a magnificent room in the Moorish style. Here, the king withdrew to celebrate his birthdays and name days in total solitude. Each year, on August 25, a memorial mass is still held here for King Ludwig II.

Neuschwanstein

The king announced the construction of the new castle of Hohenschwangau—its name was changed to Neuschwanstein in 1886, the year of Ludwig's death—in a letter to his friend Richard Wagner: "I intend to rebuild the old ruined castle of Hohenschwangau near the Pöllat Gorge. The style will follow that of the original castles of the German knights, and I must confess to you, I greatly look forward to living there. The castle will have a number of guest rooms with magnificent views of the majestic Säuling mountain." Neuschwanstein is the architectural monument dedicated to the friendship between Ludwig and the composer. Built in honor of Wagner, Ludwig saw it as "a worthy temple for the divine friend, who has bestowed upon mankind unique salvation and true blessing," as he wrote to Wagner in May 1868. What resulted is a veritable fairy tale in stone, basically a series of architectural

Richard Wagner never saw Neuschwanstein, although the castle was built in homage to him and his work. Not until February 13, 1933, the fiftieth anniversary of the composer's death—that is, already under the auspices of the National Socialists—did the first concert take place in the Singer's Hall, illuminated by the glow of 600 candles.

stage settings. The expertise of scenery designers was called for. The stage designs created by Angelo II Quaglio for the 1867 productions of *Lohengrin* and *Tannhäuser* in Munich, as well as preliminary designs by stage painter Christian Jank, were translated into construction plans by the court architect Eduard von Riedel, who was succeeded by Georg Dollmann in 1874. The king was involved in every decision, down to the last detail. The courtyard, passages, rooms and the paintings on the walls all make

reference to the great operas of Wagner. Even as it was being built, the castle increasing became a religious building for Ludwig, a "fortress of the Holy Grail." The throne room in Neuschwanstein resembles a stage set for a production of *Parsifal*, while the singer's hall, modeled after the hall in the castle at Wartburg near Eisenach, resembles the stage design for *Tannhäuser*. The king's bedroom was inspired by the nuptial chamber in *Lohengrin*.

The location of Neuschwanstein by no means allows it to be a reclusive idyll. Rather, it is a romantic castle, uniquely set on the rugged cliffs above the steep and wild depths of the Pöllat Gorge and visible for miles around. On dark nights, the king loved to step out on the Marienbrücke, the bridge over the steep valley, as candles were lighted in the singer's hall so

57 Neuschwanstein Castle near Füssen—today one of the most frequented and internationally known attractions in Germany.

that the king could revel in the gleaming splendor.

Herrenchiemsee

The third, and probably most magnificent, of Ludwig's palaces is Herrenchiemsee Castle; it is certainly the largest. He acquired the island in Lake Chiemsee on September 26, 1873, for 350,000 gold-marks. It took another five years, however, before the foundation stone was laid. Herrenchiemsee is a "hall of fame" in which Ludwig II desired to celebrate the memory of Louis XIV.

Herrenchiemsee was modeled after the French king's Versailles and built to scale, including the corner rooms, the hall of war and hall of peace, and was equipped with 52 candelabras, 33 chandeliers, tubs with orange trees, vases and benches. When Ludwig finally viewed the completed hall of mirrors, which at 328 feet (98 m) is

58   Marienbrücke. The 115-foot (35-m) high bridge across the Pöllat Gorge, inaugurated in 1842 under Crown Prince Maximilian, was named after his wife Marie. Ludwig II replaced the original wooden bridge with a filigree iron construction by Heinrich Gerber.

59   Hall of Mirrors at Herren-   ▶
chiemsee Castle, modeled after Versailles, France.

even longer than its prototype in Versailles, he compared it with French engravings of Louis XIV's masterpiece, only to notice to his great chagrin that two paintings had been hung on the wrong sides of the wall. He also felt the colors were too pale.

The architect of the castle, Ritter von Brandl, had his hands full once the monarch started to observe the progress of the work, although these visits began only in the autumn of 1881. A small wagon drawn by a locomotive was installed to transport the king across the island. Ludwig, always impatient, continually made new suggestions. At times as many as 300 people worked on the building, and when nightfall came early, the site was lit with torches so the work could continue by night.

Herrenchiemsee was conceived as a monument to monarchy, rather than a building to be lived in. Ludwig stayed there only once, for a single week, when it was completed in 1883. As in Linderhof, there is also a "magic table" with a hoist mechanism in the dining room at Herrenchiemsee. During this last visit, when he was accompanied by only a few servants and his furrier Hesselschwerdt, the entire castle was illuminated; more that 2,000 wax candles brightened the Hall of Mirrors as though hundreds of guests were expected. The

castle would have had room enough for them—not just for a lonely king.

Today, Herrenchiemsee Castle houses the King Ludwig II Museum, containing numerous exhibits, from his christening robe to his death mask, which was made by Professor E. Eberl.

In the vestibule of the castle, the visitor is greeted by a large bronze peacock. Together with the swan, the peacock represents the two determining themes that controlled the king's imagination: the age of the Bourbons and the Orient, which he knew intimately, but only from books. Toward the end of his life, Ludwig became enthusiastic about Chinese court ceremonies and as late as 1886 thought about erecting a Chinese castle modeled after the Imperial Winter Palace in Peking at the remote Plan Lake near Linderhof.

However, when building debts had mounted to several million goldmarks and the king received no further loans, all construction was halted. On January 26, 1886, Ludwig implored Interior Minister von Freilitzsch, "Because of the extremely desolate state of my finances, which has led to the interruption of my building projects which are so infinitely important to me, the main source of joy in my life is gone! In comparison, everything else is meaningless. I therefore command you to make the utmost efforts to raise money to bring about the fulfillment of my most heartfelt desire, and to silence any opposing voices. In so doing give me the gift of life anew."

In 1885, confrontations began between the king and

60   The hoist for the "magic table" at Herrenchiemsee Castle.

Prince Luitpold and his Cabinet Secretaries Lutz and Crailsheim over the royal building debts. Ludwig waited a long
time, until March 1886, to inform his mother of his difficulties. She immediately offered to give her son her jewelry,
worth several million marks, in order to redeem his debts.
Ludwig was deeply moved by her gesture and thanked her
profoundly, but countered, "I beg you to rather keep everything. Through some kind of manipulations it must be possible for the cabinet to bring matters back on track." Ludwig
held Cabinet Secretary Gresser responsible for the financial
disaster. On April 21, the monarch confided to his mother
that he was very unhappy, because the problem seemed to
become ever more sad and serious.

The queen mother was of the opinion that the state
treasury of Bavaria should pick up the king's debts. All along,
the king had paid the building costs for his castles Neuschwanstein, Linderhof, and Herrenchiemsee from his private
purse, and the cabinet understandably saw no reason to alter
matters at this point. The king in any case received an annual
income of 4.5 million goldmarks. By 1886, his debts had
reached 14 million marks, that is, three times his annual
income.

The impending financial disaster might well have been
averted if all construction on the buildings had been stopped
at once and financial experts had worked out a long-term
solution. Instead, the cabinet ministers, the royal princes and
the psychiatrists denounced the king's attitude toward money
as "a symptom of a mental disease"—and by so doing, they
"caused the dramatic developments which eventually led to
the King's death." Once progress on the castles was forcibly
halted, Ludwig's life had no meaning. Whereas Maximilian II
Joseph and Ludwig I had built primarily for the public, the

How sad that everything is worse than you write! In Munich, I heard how
sorry everyone is, how fond the citizens of Munich are of you, how much
everyone wants to help. To see you there again ... that's what they long
for! If construction ceases for some time ... it would be easy to get help ...
I am glad to hear how they carry you in their hearts—I did not expect it
from the common people! ... Everyone sees how you have been deceived
and kept uninformed about how matters were being mishandled.
                        Queen Mother Marie to Ludwig II, April 25, 1886

castles and palaces of Ludwig II were so exclusively reserved for the king himself that he even contemplated the idea of having them destroyed after his death. Indeed, during his lifetime, the castles were kept hermetically sealed; he had never made provision for an entrance for visitors. Today, visitors from all over the world come to see and admire them and the parks, and thereby contribute to their maintenance.

61 Herrenchiemsee. View of the garden facade of the castle with the Latona Fountain in the foreground.

Prince Otto, the Later King Otto— Unfit to Reign

Prince Otto, who resembled his mother in appearance, was the most cheerful person in the family. Ludwig and Otto grew up together; they played and fought as siblings do. Otto also received the same education as his older brother and, beginning in 1866, he studied history, social studies, and aesthetics at the University of Munich. Otto enjoyed opera as much as his brother, but preferred the music of Jacques Offenbach to the operas of Richard Wagner. He adored the theater—and the ladies of the ballet corps. From early on Otto had been reminded that "Crown Prince Ludwig is always first."

On several occasions, the two princes attended church celebrations or public events together. In August 1864, having accompanied their mother to the Swiss Chalet, Ludwig inscribed in the guest book in rhymed lines:

How glad I am to greet
   you once again,
Peaceful house, after such a
   long time! –
Content, I welcome you, serenely floating brook,

62   Prince Otto of Bavaria in a
general's uniform. Photograph,
1873.

You trees and mountains far and near.
Here, I breathe your brisk air,
Take pleasure in the clear blue sky.
Flowers welcome me with sweet fragrance,
Fresh morning dew sparkles on their leaves.
I tell this wonderful landscape
That I wish to stay for a long time. Ludwig

Otto, on the other hand, rhymed shortly and briefly:

Just now Count Taxis brought us
With a waiter's skill,
Coffee and butter for breakfast. Otto

While the king often pretended to be sick or indisposed in order to avoid attending royal balls, Otto took genuine pleasure in these events.

The young prince had two great passions—hunting and traveling. His love of hunting was in fact extraordinary. Whenever he accompanied his mother to Salzburg, Berchtesgaden, or Tyrol, he always went on a chamois hunt. The queen did not entirely approve of Otto's predilection. She once complained to her son Ludwig that Otto went hunting before dinner almost every day; "Otherwise, he does practically nothing."

Otto pursued a military career, becoming a lieutenant in 1861, a first lieutenant in 1864, and a captain in the royal infantry regiment in 1866. When he came of age, he received an annual salary of 80,000 florins, and his brother accepted him into the Order of the Knights of St. George.

During the German War of 1866, Prince Otto arrived at the Franconian headquarters of his great uncle, Prince Karl, on

He [Otto] is a very ordinary man without the slightest appreciation for art and beauty. He spends his entire days hunting, often in the company of my dull and unimaginative cousin, and attends the Aktientheater at night, where he is especially enthusiastic about the ballet.

From a letter to Cosima von Bülow,
January 24, 1867

June 21. After the peace treaty with Prussia he received the Knight's Cross, First Class, and at the end of the Franco-Prussian War, he was decorated with the Iron Cross. Ultimately he became the commander of the 5th Calvary Regiment, which he reviewed on August 12, 1867, in its quarters in the garrison town of Speyer.

In contrast to his brother Ludwig, Otto enjoyed traveling. He often accompanied his mother on her travels, for instance, in April 1865 to Schwerin and Berlin, and together they visited Hamburg and Kiel. In September 1866, he took a five-week trip to northern Italy; and in both 1864 and 1868, together with Ludwig II, he joined the Russian czar and czarina at Kissingen. Ludwig and Otto visited Wartburg Castle near Eisenach, and together they experienced the triumphant conclusion to their parents' tour of Franconia in Nuremberg. A long journey to the Orient followed, during which Otto became indisposed, so that he subsequently went to Italy to recover. Together with his mother he often took over state obligations for his retiring brother and presented himself to the people in Munich at public receptions, celebrations or parades. On April 1, 1868, the king issued the following order: "I deem it appropriate that greater feasts shall once again take place at the court. Because of my illness I will not be able to attend them myself in the near future and therefore ask Prince Otto to stand in my stead at these dinners in the winter garden; courtiers, ministers, state and imperial representatives should be in-

63   Queen Mother Marie with her sons Ludwig and Otto on the entrance stairs of Hohenschwangau Castle. Photograph by Joseph Albert, ca. 1860.

vited." Once again, Ludwig had shifted responsibilities over to his brother.

Otto loved gala events. On February 8, 1869, he accompanied Ludwig in the royal coach to the Marienplatz in Munich, where the festival of the Metzgersprung took place every year, a graduation ceremony for the apprentices of the butchers guild: they were tossed into the Fish Fountain and declared to be journeymen. Otto amused himself greatly. He also loved to attend the Octoberfest, whereas his brother was present only five times in the 21 years of his reign.

Otto experienced one event in his mother's life very vividly: her conversion to Catholicism on October 12, 1874. After her husband's sudden death in 1864, the gregarious queen was transformed into a deeply mourning widow. Her sons were very caring, but over the years she became increasingly more lonely. When it became clear that her son Otto was mentally ill, the Catholic clergy suggested to "the unhappy mother that her son would be healed if she converted to the Catholic faith." The influence of her favorite niece, Therese, on Prince Otto must also have been significant. Therese belonged to the Catholic conservative circle at court and exerted a strong influence on the appointment of church officials in Munich.

Ever since participating in the Franco-Prussian War in 1870, Prince Otto had exhibited signs of mental fragility. Aa early as 1867, according to reports of the usually well-informed Prussian Ambassador Baron von Werthern, rumors about Otto's mental illness began to spread, raising the question of whether Otto should be excluded from the succession to the throne. The Prussian ambassador reported to Bismarck that Otto regularly suffered from a "cold fever;" the royal family could not avert its eyes from the bouts of restlessness

---

Ludwig's and Otto's reactions to the **conversion of their mother to Catholicism** varied. Ludwig chose a very unlikely place—a typical grand reception in the royal tent on the Festival Grounds—to inform the Princes Luitpold and Adalbert, as well as the Apostolic delegate, not only of his mother's conversion,

but also of his own disapproval of the step.

Otto's response was entirely different. Writing to his cousin Ludwig Ferdinand on October 20, 1874, he said "I am sure you were delighted that my mother converted to the Catholic faith!—It is a sign of God's grace! Right after the conversion,

and anxiety suffered by the then 19-year-old prince. By the end of 1865, the queen mother had already started to consult with doctors and had her son examined; his restlessness was diagnosed as a sort of "youthful disorder" which would pass in time.

As Otto became seriously ill and Ludwig increasingly retreated from official obligations and, indeed, from reality, the Austrian Empress Elisabeth (Sisi) took up the defense of her "royal cousin" Ludwig and inquired in detail about her cousin Otto's disease. She felt quite drawn to people who had crossed "the border between normalcy and madness." Elisabeth was interested in "madhouses" and wanted to know how the "mad" were treated, although one could hardly speak of treatment at that time. The empress finally determined to visit a mental institution in Munich and asked Queen Mother Marie to accompany her. The empress's lady-in-waiting, Countess Marie Festetics, described this visit of 1874 as follows: "The empress was pale and serious; the queen, however, who has two mentally ill sons—God have mercy—was amused and laughed." It is entirely possible that the queen's reaction was wholly misinterpreted and that her "laughter" was rather an expression of embarrassment and helplessness.

Otto's bouts of confusion became increasingly serious. As a result, by November 1871, even the royal family no longer regarded him fit for a succession to the throne.

At the king's command, Prince Otto received discrete treatment at Nymphenburg Castle. The adjutants and servants were ordered to deal with him as though he were completely normal. More and more, the prince was cut off from the outer world, an isolation increased by his fits of anxiety. One such attack, for instance, was directed against his former

---

one could see the inner peace and serenity—God bless her forever. The ceremony at the church of Waltenhof [near Hohenschwangau] was uplifting! The sun was shining brightly, the music was beautiful!— Bishop von Haneberg von Speyer preached very well!—Dean von Reindl of the cathedral wrote me a

very nice letter in this regard which made me very happy!"

adjutant, Count Dürckheim-Montmartin, on whom he believed to see the head of a devil. Although he still enjoyed some clear moments, as when his second adjutant, Baron Karl Reisner von Lichtenstein, shared society gossip with him, the prince eventually fell into complete silence.

At Christmas 1871, Ludwig and his mother agreed that under no circumstances would Otto be sent to a psychiatric clinic; instead, he would remain on the family estates and removed as much as possible from the public eye. Otto spent most of his time at Nymphenburg. However, until 1874, he was still capable of accompanying his mother to the mountains and of attending mass with her.

An embarrassing incident took place on May 27, 1875, during the Feast of Corpus Christi service. Escaping his guardians in Nymphenburg, Otto stormed into the nave of the Church of Our Lady in Munich, fell to his knees at the altar and prayed for the forgiveness of his sins. Apparently, he was tortured by the illusion that he would be damned forever because he had once been unworthy while receiving the Catholic sacrament of Communion. Over time, his lifestyle became increasingly irregular. Soon he refused to get out of bed for days on end, and refused altogether to eat.

Between April 1883 and his death in October 1916, Otto was a permanent resident of Fürstenried Castle. The attending doctors, who had been observing him since May 1871, diagnosed a "deterioration of his nervous system" resulting from his unrestrained moral conduct. According to reports by Franz Karl Müller, the assistant of Bernhard von Gudden, the medical diagnosis of June 1886 confirmed "mental disturbance, pronounced states of exaltation, depression, hallucinations, compulsive movements, and delusions." Not until Ludwig's death in October 1886 did the public learn through

---

64 Therese (1850–1925), known fondly to the family as "little Therese," was only 13 years old when her mother Auguste, who had married the later Prince Regent Luitpold, died of a lung disease at the age of 39. Therese grew up under the care of her sister-in-law Marie and developed into an extraordinary personality. She traveled throughout Europe, Asia Minor, the West Indies, and North and South America as a researcher. Her scientific achievements led to her appointment as an honorary member of the Bavarian Academy of Sciences, and she received an honorary doctorate from the

the press that Otto I, the official successor to the throne, was suffering from "madness" or "paranoia."

His mother never tired of visiting her son at Fürstenried. Indeed, she wrote no letter to Ludwig in which she did not mention his brother. It might well happen that Otto was sleeping when Marie arrived at Fürstenried, and Marie, after long hours of waiting, had to return to Munich without having spoken to her son; she never allowed him to be awakened. In the end, Otto was rarely capable of recognizing even his mother.

Marie's last hand-written letter, dated December 31, 1888, and addressed to her niece, Princess Therese, included the sentence, "I am glad that you visit Otto." As it became more difficult for Marie to hold a pen, her last communication with her niece was a telegram on April 12, 1889, in which she expressed her gratitude that Therese and her father, Prince-Regent Luitpold, had visited Otto at Fürstenried, and thanked her for the "cheerful news about Otto and the snowbells."

In the estate of Princess Therese, a journal was found which the queen mother had received from a priest from Elbigenalp on December 31, 1888. It contains a note written on the evening before Otto's birthday, that is, on April 26, 1889: "May God bless and keep him for us. ... Champagne,

University of Munich. Although the princess was never married, she had one bittersweet love affair: She was very attached to her cousin Otto, who always sent her cheerful letters and postcards from his travels. When she first arrived at Hohenschwangau Castle as a girl, she was introduced to "an existence filled with poetry, romanticism, and the preservation of the old German sagas, [opening] a new world for me." As she finally overcame her sorrow over her mother's death and perhaps even hoped to find a companion for life in Otto, she noticed that he was ill. Her love for him thus remained unfulfilled.

with which we toasted his Majesty, the King." On Otto's birthday itself she noted, "Hail, our King, hail! God bless his Majesty, the King!" After the queen mother's death in May, Therese was probably the only relative who continued to concern herself with her sick cousin.

King Otto I was legally "dethroned" on November 5, 1913, according to a constitutional amendment introduced by his cousin, Prince Leopold, who, as the eldest son of Luitpold, had served since 1912 as Prince-Regent. A proclamation issued on that occasion reads, "The royal house and the people have found that after 27 years of a deep affliction, His Majesty, King Otto I, is unable to reign due to severe illness." Otto died of appendicitis in 1916 at the age of 69. Along with his brother Ludwig II, he was laid to rest in the family grave in St. Michael's Church in Munich. In contrast to Ludwig's tomb, which is often strewn with bouquets, Otto's is only rarely graced with attention.

The King's Last Year

"Yes, I was a fairy-tale King. ..."

The last year of the king's life was characterized by his extreme aversion to people and a desperate search for financial resources that would allow him to complete construction on his palaces. In a conversation with Prince Luitpold, Ludwig's uncle, on February 5, 1886, Cabinet Secretary Johann Lutz broached the subject of appointing Luitpold Prince-Regent, under the condition that he would accept the present cabinet. Such a move required a psychiatric evaluation which stated that the king was unfit to reign. In March 1886, Lutz discussed their plan with psychiatrist Johann Bernhard Aloys von Gudden, professor of psychiatry at the University of Munich since 1872, and the director of a psychiatric institution in Upper Bavaria.

Just 40 years old, the king was not a healthy man. He could tolerate only the presence of his most trusted servants, who were familiar with his

65   The changing face of a king:
Ludwig II in 1867, 1872 and 1883.
Photographs by Joseph Albert.

attitudes and habits. In fact, Ludwig was by then surrounded by people who supported his grandiose plans and unrealistic ideas for reasons of personal profit. As a result, disappointments were inevitable, for Ludwig II was no longer able to come to terms with the personal weaknesses and shortcomings of those around him, whom he had idealized. Extremely generous to those he loved, he could be equally harsh against those who had lost his favor, whether servants or knights.

Ludwig's final meeting with his mother took place on October 14, 1885, the day before her sixtieth birthday. As a birthday surprise, Ludwig wanted to show her his nearly completed castle, Neuschwanstein. The steward of Hohenschwangau reported in his chronicle, "On 14 October, the King arrived from Linderhof at 11:00 P.M. to congratulate his mother on her sixtieth birthday. October 15: Weibl celebrated mass at 9:00 A.M. in the chapel; lunch at noon; at 2:00 P.M. Her Majesty received the King's congratulations and precious gifts. At 3:00 P.M. both Majesties visited the new building and the Queen Mother admired the magnificent interiors of the rooms for the first time. Then they departed for the Swiss Chalet in Böckenau where, in the meantime, the rest of the guests had arrived from Hohenschwangau and dinner was served at 4:00 P.M. The party returned to Hohenschwangau at 9:30 P.M. On October 16, at 5:00 P.M., the King departed to return to Linderhof." Mother and son were never to meet again.

On Good Friday of the year of his death, Ludwig visited Füssen, in order to pray at the 14 stations of the cross. His mother wrote to him to express her joy at his magnificent Easter presents, and gave her son her best wishes.

The king often suffered from toothaches, but was unwilling to have his bad teeth replaced by artificial dentures. As a result, he often turned to strong painkillers; in addition,

Oh, that your days might be happier than up until now! I pray to God daily and have had masses said for you! Tomorrow is Otto's birthday. It has been so long since we have celebrated it together!   *Easter letter of Queen Mother Marie to Ludwig II, 1886*

to combat his insomnia, he took sleeping drugs, including opium. Soon he was dependent on both these drugs as well as alcohol.

The end of Ludwig's reign

By 1886, Ludwig had withdrawn from the real world to such a degree that he was hardly able to perform the tasks of government. On top of this, his building debts and his submersion in an ever more fantastic world of ideas had disrupted his relationship with his cabinet. It is thus hardly surprising that those who carried the political responsibility in Munich sought ways to remove the king. In view of the psychological problems of Ludwig's brother, dethronement on the grounds of mental illness seemed an attractive argument. It is a known fact that four eminent psychiatrists—von Gudden, Hagen, Grashey, and Hubrich—declared the king mad, without even one of them ever examining him. Von Gudden even went so far as to diagnose paranoia. According to the Munich psychoanalyst Wolfgang Schmidbauer, "The experts' report contains a long list of negative statements and excludes any positive comment. For political reasons, not even the remnants of a healthy personality were to be ascribed to Ludwig." In any case, the evaluation was essentially intended to prove that the king was unfit for his office.

66   Ludwig II in the robe of a Grand Master of the Order of the Knights of St. Hubertus. Painting by Franz Lenbach, 1880.

At 3:00 A.M. on June 10, 1886, a state commission appeared in Neuschwanstein to arrest the king. Headed by Baron Krafft von Crailsheim, the commission consisted of Count Törring, Dr. Rumpler, Lieutenant Colonel Maximilian von Washington, and Count Maximilian von Holnstein. Also present were Dr. Gudden and his assistant, Dr. Müller, accompanied by several guards of an insane asylum. The group arrived at the hotel in Hohenschwangau around midnight. They ate a seven-course dinner and drank 40 quarts of beer and ten bottles of champagne. After the meal, Count Holnstein spoke with Ludwig's personal coachman, Franz Osterholz, in the stables. Osterholz managed to make his way over secret paths to warn the king of the impending arrival of the commission. Immediately, the castle was hermetically sealed, and police corps and fire brigades of the neighboring villages were put on alert. The guards prevented the commission from entering the castle. The men returned to Hohenschwangau with their mission incomplete. Although the king ordered the members of the commission to be arrested and locked up at Neuschwanstein, the commission managed to return to Munich on the following day.

The only remaining person in the vicinity of the king whom he trusted was his servant Alfons Weber. Referring to him as his "last follower," Ludwig handed over to him all his remaining money, a sum of 1,200 marks, as well as a precious piece of jewelry from his hat worth 2,500 marks.

Ludwig must have realized that a new commission would soon arrive. Waiting desperately, he was at first calm and peaceful, but as night fell, Ludwig began to drink—a whole bottle of rum spiced with cloves and a bottle of champagne. The excessive amount of alcohol made him aggressive and nervous.

I do believe in the immortality of the soul and in God's justice. ... To be catapulted down from the highest level of life into nothingness—that is a life lost; I cannot bear it. That they take away my crown I could bear, but that they have declared me mentally ill, I will not survive. I could not tolerate the same fate as my poor brother Otto, whom any guard can order around, whom they threaten to beat if he does not obey. ... May my blood be upon all those who have betrayed me! Luit-

After the first failed attempt to arrest the king, Ludwig's adjutant, Count Alfred von Dürckheim-Montmartin, set out hastily from Munich for Neuschwanstein. His advice to the king was identical to that of Bismarck, whom Dürckheim had telegrammed for advice: the king should immediately return to Munich and present himself to the people. Ludwig refused both Dürckheim's advice as well as the suggestion from one of his friends to escape to nearby Tyrol in northern Italy. Thus fate took its course. In the meantime, the newly appointed Prince-Regent Luitpold had informed all the police stations in the vicinity of Füssen that the king had been deposed on the grounds of mental illness. Ludwig feared a battle with the gendarmes who had been sent in from Munich to replace the locals and wrote, "I do not want any bloodshed on my behalf."

In a state of resignation, the king played with the idea of suicide. Even his most intimate friends feared he would jump off the castle's tower. But then he changed his mind: "Drowning is a nicer death. No mutilation. But falling from a great height. ..."

During the night of June 11 to 12, the second commission arrived at Neuschwanstein and appeared before the king. The medical doctor approached him, "Your Majesty,

67   One of the last photographs of Ludwig II. Joseph Albert, 1883.

pold, a fine relative! He takes the power and has me arrested! He is not a Prince-Regent, he is a Rebel Prince!
        *Ludwig II to his servant,
    Alfons Weber, June 10, 1886*

this is the saddest obligation I have ever fulfilled. Your Majesty has been evaluated by four psychiatric experts and based on their recommendation Prince Luitpold has taken over the political responsibilities on your behalf. I have the order to accompany Your Majesty to Berg Castle, in fact tonight. If Your Majesty gives the order, the coach will be ready at 4:00 A.M." The king shouted in torment, "What do you want? What is happening?" Then he was taken in charge by the guards and taken to his bedroom, which smelled strongly of brandy. There Dr. Gudden introduced the members of the commission one by one, mentioning that he had had the honor of an audience with the king in 1874. At the time, twelve years earlier, Ludwig had entrusted Gudden with the treatment of his brother Otto. The king replied, "Yes, I recall precisely," inquired about his brother's health and then asked, "How can you declare me mentally ill when you have neither examined nor spoken to me?" Dr. Gudden replied that the documentation showed overwhelming evidence. It was obvious, however, that the report was based not on medical evidence, but rather on political arguments which had been gathered by Prince-Regent Luitpold.

The final act

On June 12, the Saturday before Pentecost, three coaches arrived in the courtyard of Berg Castle at 12:15 P.M. In the first coach sat Dr. Müller and two medical attendants, in the second the king alone had been enclosed, and in the third were the chief of police and two additional caretakers. In Seeshaupt at Lake Starnberg, where the horses were exchanged for the last time, the king asked for a glass of water,

On June 10, 1886, **Prince Luitpold** took over the reign from his two nephews, who had been declared mentally ill. Luitpold was born on March 12, 1821, the third son of Ludwig I and was the younger brother of Maximilian II Joseph and Otto I of Greece. After his death on December 12, 1912, his oldest son, Ludwig, succeeded him as Prince-Regent. One year later, after Otto's dethronement, he took the crown as the last king of Bavaria, Ludwig III. On November 7 to 8, 1918, he in turn was forced to resign by a rebellion led by Kurt Eisner. He died on October 18, 1921, in Sárvár, Hungary.

which the post office clerk handed to him respectfully. The ride had taken 18 hours.

It must have been extremely humiliating for the king to notice that in the castle which he knew so well all door handles had been removed, the windows had been secured with iron bars, and the doors drilled through with a hole for the purpose of observation—all measures which must have been a long time in preparation. After lunch, at around 3:00 P.M., the humiliated man lay down to rest. When he woke up at midnight, dressed only in his nightshirt and socks, he searched for his clothes, but the guards refused to give them to him. At dawn, he fell asleep again. He received Dr. Gudden and his son-in-law, Dr. Grashey, the following morning. They rejected Ludwig's request to attend mass on Pentecost Sunday. Between 11:00 A.M. and 12:15 P.M., Dr. Gudden accompanied the king on an initial walk. Then the king had a lonely lunch, followed by further conversations with the staff comptroller Zanders. Some time later, Dr. Müller arrived. At 4:30 P.M., the king asked for something to eat, against the advice of Dr. Gudden. He seemed to be very hungry and drank a glass of beer, two glasses of spiced wine, three glasses of Rhine wine, and two small glasses of brandy. After the meal, he reminded Dr. Gudden that they had agreed on another walk. Dr. Gudden, who had no desire to go, said to Baron von Washington, "I wish the King would spare me the walk! The man is so tiresome with his many questions!" He telegraphed Lutz in Munich, "Here, everything is working out wonderfully." He left Washington saying, "Until 8, for supper!" Against all common sense, Gudden decided to accompany the king without the guards.

By 8:00 P.M., he and the king had not returned. Dr. Müller was alarmed, especially because it had begun to rain heavily.

Much too early he had to leave	They bound you swiftly
His beloved palace:	With bandages and chloroform,
Neuschwanstein, proud castle,	You had to leave your castle,
You were the King's dearest treasure!	And can never again return!
Much too early he had to leave,	They took you to Berg Castle
They took him away by force,	During the last night of your life.
Like barbarians they treated you,	You were sentenced to death
Led you away through the forest.	In the very same night.

He informed the police, who sent all available men on a search with lamps and torches. Not until around 10:00 P.M. did a courtier notice something dark floating on the surface of the lake. It was the king's jacket and overcoat. The court officer Rottenhöfer found the king's umbrella and the guard Schneller discovered Ludwig's hat. Nearby lay Gudden's hat as well. About half an hour later, they sighted the bodies of the former monarch and the doctor floating in shallow water approximately 65 to 70 feet (20 to 25 m) from shore. Despite unclear evidence in the water, it can be assumed that Ludwig II tried to commit suicide and that Dr. Gudden attempted to hold him back. Gudden, much smaller than the king, must have been at a disadvantage in the struggle, so that he fell in the water and drowned. Thus, the life of the Bavarian king ended under tragic—and still unresolved—circumstances on

68 The king's last walk with the psychiatrist Dr. Bernhard von Gudden in the park of Berg Castle on June 13, 1886. Engraving based on a water color by Heinrich Breling.

69 The discovery of the king's ▶ corpse at Lake Starnberg. Engraving from *L'Illustration*, Paris, June 26, 1886.

June 13, 1886, and at the same time, the "myth of Ludwig II" was born!

The two corpses were laid out on the first floor of the castle, Dr. Gudden in the former living room, and Ludwig in the queen mother's bedroom.

As soon as in the early morning hours of June 14, the citizens of Munich were informed of the king's death by posters and several newspaper reports. The news spread like wildfire first through the city and then throughout the country. The news also traveled by telegrams. On June 14, 1886, at 5:30 P.M., Baron Washington dispatched Telegram No. 68, not to the queen mother directly, but to her chief lady-in-waiting.

How did Marie herself learn of her son's death? At the time, the widowed queen was ill in Elbigenalp. Her niece, Princess Therese, the person whom Marie trusted most highly next to her confessor, had the difficult task of bringing her the sad news. Accompanied by the priest, Therese entered the queen mother's room. The priest read a particular passage from the Bible, repeating it three times. After he had finished, the queen mother asked her lady-in-waiting, Julie von der Mühle, if something had happened to her son. When she remained silent, she turned to Princess Therese and asked whether her son was dead. Therese then nodded silently. The queen mother cried bitterly and collapsed.

The next day, the newspapers in Bavaria carried a false report that the queen mother had suddenly died, but the story was retracted the following day. The sorrow over her son's death affected Marie so profoundly that she was confined to her bed for four weeks. Thus she never saw her dead son. She received a very personal letter from Crown Prince Frederick William of Prussia: "Today, I saw your beloved son for the last time, after not having seen him for 15 years. Peace and serenity lay on his features, whose beauty not even death could alter. Large crowds of people from all different classes of society came to say farewell to their king and the stream continues." A lock of Ludwig's hair was brought to his mother in Elbingenalp. She wrote on the envelope, which contained it, in her own hand, "Ludwig's hair, June 1886."

In the night from June 14 to 15, the king's body was transported from Berg Castle to the royal residence in Munich. After an extensive autopsy, the body was embalmed and then laid in state in the All Saints' Church in Munich, thus giving the citizens of Bavaria three days to say a last farewell to their king, who appeared as if he had peacefully fallen asleep. His body was clad in the black robe of the Order of the Knights of Saint Hubertus, his sword in his left hand, and a small bouquet of jasmine sent by Empress Elisabeth of Austria in his right.

On Saturday June 9, around 11:30 A.M., the bells of every church in Munich rang in mourning for an entire hour. Then the wagon carrying the king's coffin set out from the royal residence to the king's final resting place, St. Michael's Church. The streets were crowded with mourners. In front of the church, Dean Ritter von Türck and the court clergy received the casket. It was carried solemnly through the nave to the

70   King Ludwig II lying in state. ▶
Colored photograph, 1886.

choir where it was put down and covered with wreaths and flower bouquets. Later, the casket was placed in a preliminary sarcophagus, sealed by the minister of the royal house, and carried into the crypt. Four months later, the casket of King Ludwig II was transferred to its final neo-classical sarcophagus.

Mourning the dead king

In a letter to her aunt, the queen mother, Therese wrote, "[You know] that I am attached to you deep in my soul and with a truly childlike love. So you will understand how deeply I feel for you and share your suffering over the heavy loss you have to bear." She pointed out that for months she had been tortured by premonitions that something might happen to the family, also fearing for her father, Luitpold, who had taken the incapacitation of the king very hard and had tried to postpone it as long as possible. "While papa is burdened by

the sad course of events, because he was forced to a sacrifice that changed his life entirely, your suffering is much deeper, your motherly heart has been affected most painfully. My thoughts and feelings are most of all with you! When the Lord imposes such suffering, He certainly also provides the strength to bear it!" Although she could not be physically close to her aunt, she was with her in prayer. "The whole event is like a terrible nightmare whose reality I cannot believe!"

On August 25, 1886, both the birthday and name day of her son, the queen mother ordered a memorial mass for Ludwig at St. Michael's Church in Munich. Finally, on September 22, she was strong enough to visit his sarcophagus in the crypt, accompanied by her lady-in-waiting, Countess Julie von der Mühle. At the portal, she was greeted by the priest who had earlier celebrated the mass. Marie laid down a large cross of edelweiss and white roses. As she left the church crying bitterly the people bowed to her silently. Marie then traveled to be with Otto—officially the king but unable to reign—in Fürstenried. Mourning deeply, she went to Berg Castle and walked through the rooms so much loved by Ludwig, and then visited the site of the tragedy at the lake. She planted some ivy and returned to Hohenschwangau on the same day. Her sixty-first birthday on October 18, 1886, was the saddest of her life.

Prince Leopold of Bavaria, the son of Prince-Regent Luitpold and nephew of the queen, noted in his memoirs, "It was terrible for the poor queen mother, who is already so sorely tired. However, the noble woman, indeed, never held anything against my father or any of us. She extended to us— but especially to my sister [Therese]—unflagging familial love and care. My dear mother-in-law, who at the time was

On June 10, 1886, **Marie Valérie** noted in her diary that Ludwig, having been declared mentally ill, had been forced to resign, and that her Uncle Luitpold had taken over as Prince-Regent. Princess Gisela, Luitpold's wife, had brought Marie Valérie's mother, Empress Elisabeth of Austria, the news of the king's death with a stony expression on her face. The young princess confided her thoughts on this blow of fate to her diary: "Mama, on the other hand, sees this terrible event not only as the sad end of a unique king, but also mourns the friend of her youth. Filled with memories of beautiful hours, she is

visiting her mother in Feldafing, was very hard hit by the loss." Prince Leopold's mother-in-law was the Empress Elisabeth of Austria, called Sisi, who together with her youngest daughter, Grand Duchess Marie Valérie, was staying at Feldafing.

On June 22, 1886, Empress Elisabeth and her daughter arranged for a festive requiem mass to be held for Ludwig II in the village church in Feldafing. The coat of arms of the House of Wittelsbach hung over the altar, which was covered with black draping. The large catafalque in front of the altar was covered with oak leaves and wreaths of jasmine and roses; the coat of arms was wound with rhododendron. On the following day, the empress drove to Munich in order to lay a wreath on the king's sarcophagus in St. Michael's Church. Following that visit she told her daughter she preferred knowing that the king rested peacefully there among his forefathers than that he would have lived under Luitpold's reign, which he would have hated.

In her diary, Marie Valérie often compared her mother to King Ludwig II of Bavaria, who had been her soul mate. On March 13, 1902, many years after the king's death, she spoke with his former adjutant, Count Alfred Dürckheim-Montmartin, who had had been present during Ludwig's apprehension in 1886, at a festive dinner at the House of Thurn and Taxis. He confirmed that the empress had at the time wished to speak to her royal cousin, but had been discouraged from doing so.

Since the 18th century, it had been a tradition to bury the hearts of the regents of the House of Wittelsbach in urns near the image of the Sacred Heart in the Altötting Chapel, a Bavarian shrine. As the hearts of his grandparents and parents before him, Ludwig's heart found its last rest there. The urn

now completely disturbed by her sorrow. ... Perhaps Mama is wrong when she says the king was no fool, but rather a loner who lived in (different) ideal worlds. ... When I went to pray with Mama the other night, she was lying on the floor. I screamed loudly because I thought she had seen something and clung to her so anxiously that we eventually had to laugh. Mama said she had wanted to ask God humbly and with remorse to forgive her rebellious thoughts ... and in humility to say: Jehovah, you are great, you are the God of revenge, of grace, and of wisdom."

containing Ludwig's heart, 30 inches (65 cm) high and made out of gilded silver, was set in place on August 16, 1886. The ceremony began at 5:30 A.M. with a service was conducted in the Royal Chapel in the presence of family members. Then Dean von Türck carried the black-veiled urn through a lane formed by 24 guards to the royal coach. Drawn by six horses the coach drove in a solemn procession through Munich to the train station from which it continued to its final destination, the donor's church of Altötting where the Bishop of Passau celebrated the requiem mass. In addition to the Bavarian coat of arms in gold and a metal crown, the urn bears bouquets of rhododenron and edelweiss.

To commemorate the first anniversary of her son's death, as well as his birthday and name day, in 1887 the queen mother had a wreath bearing a dedication on a black satin ribbon brought from Hohenschwangau to Munich, and requested a low mass in Ludwig's honor. In addition, she donated several memorial lights in neo-Gothic style that were dedicated to the king and placed around the edge of Starnberg Lake near the spot where his body had been found.

In June 1888, the queen mother wrote a letter to Marie Therese, wife of the later King Ludwig III, which testifies to

ERZHERZOGIN MARIE VALERIE
UND
ERZHERZOG FRANZ SALVATOR.

71   Grand Duchess Marie Valérie of Austria, daughter of Empress Elisabeth of Austria, was in Feldafing when the king died. Photograph, 1880.

the extent her strong faith helped her deal with the severe loss. "I would like to thank you and the others, especially Gisela and Therese, for your true compassion and remembrance of yesterday's difficult day of mourning. Two years have already passed. I thank God that my Ludwig is peaceful in heaven. To my joy and consolation, we held two high requiems and five holy masses for him."

In his condolences, Pope Leo XIII described Ludwig II as "[a] charming King, blessed with all of God's gifts! From his forefathers he inherited the passionate love for beauty and greatness, and a kindness that delighted his people. ... Of ideal beauty, open-hearted for everything that was uplifting and moving, he ascended to the throne, adored by his people. He was the most popular King."

72 "A tender kiss for the marble king." Postcard from the years following Ludwig's death.

Timeline

1811 *November 28*
Maximilian II Joseph of Bavaria, Ludwig's father, born

1825 *October 18*
Princess Marie von Hohenzollern, from the ruling family of Prussia, born

1837 *December 24*
Elisabeth, the future Empress of Austria, born in Munich as the fourth daughter of Max and Ludovika of Bavaria

1842 *October 12*
Princess Marie von Hohenzollern and Crown Prince Maximilian of Bavaria married in Munich

1845 *January 7*
Prince Ludwig of Bavaria, later Ludwig III, born
August 25
Hereditary Prince Otto Ludwig Friedrich Wilhelm, later Ludwig II, born in Nymphenburg Palace near Munich

1848 *March 20*
King Ludwig I of Bavaria, grandfather of Ludwig II, abdicates
March 21
Maximilian II Joseph becomes king; Ludwig becomes crown prince
April 27
Prince Otto Wilhelm Ludwig, Crown Prince Ludwig's brother, born in Nymphenburg Palace
December 2
Franz Joseph becomes Emperor of Austria

1861 *February 2*
Crown Prince Ludwig sees *Lohengrin*, his first Wagner opera

1862 *December 22*
Crown Prince Ludwig attends his first performance of Wagner's opera *Tannhäuser*

1863 *September 20*
Crown Prince Ludwig swears a constitutional oath after reaching maturity and later takes another constitutional oath in Berchtesgaden

1864 Austria and Prussia wage war against Danish King Christian IX
March 10
King Maximilian II Joseph dies in Munich; Ludwig takes the Royal Oath in the royal residence in Munich
March 14
Funeral of King Maximilian II Joseph in the Theatiner Church
March 27
The Bavarian parliament, which had been closed since 1863, re-opens. All members of parliament are invited to a royal banquet; there is a general amnesty for all participants of the revolution of 1848/49
May 4
Ludwig II meeta Richard Wagner in the royal residence in Munich
June 3
Ludwig begins his first building project: the Nibelun-

gen Corridor in the residence in Munich

June 18–July 14
Ludwig II travels to Kissingen and meets with the Austrian and Russian imperial couples

October
Richard Wagner moves into a rented house on Brienner Strasse in Munich, paid for by the king

1865 *March 28*
Empress Elizabeth of Austria comes to Munich to meet with Ludwig II

June 10
Wagner's opera *Tristan and Isolde* premiers at the Court Theater, Munich

August 27
Richard Wagner completes the draft for his opera *Parsifal*

October 18
The unshortened version of Friedrich Schiller's play *Wilhelm Tell* performed in Munich

October
Ludwig II travels to the sites of the Tell saga in Switzerland

November 11
Richard Wagner visits King Ludwig II for some days at Hohenschwangau Castle

December 10
Ludwig II is forced by all political parties to dismiss Wagner, who leaves Munich

December 13
Empress Elisabeth of Austria visits Munich

year's end
Prince Otto shows first signs of mental disorder ("youthful disturbance")

1866 *March 29*
Partial mobilization of Prussia. Prussia invades Holstein and leaves the German Federation; German

Federation declares war on Prussia

May 9
Ludwig II says he would rather resign in favor of his brother Otto than declare war

May 10
Ludwig II orders mobilization in Bavaria for June 22

May 22
Ludwig journeys to Wagner in Tribschen, Switzerland

May 27
Opening session of the state parliament in Bavaria

June 15–July 26
German War for hegemony over Germany between Prussia and Austria

June 16
German Federation attacked by Prussia; war declared

June 21
Prince Otto arrives at the headquarters of his uncle, Prince Karl, and serves as an officer

June 25
Ludwig II visits the Bavarian headquarters in Bamberg

July 3
Austria and its allies defeated at Königgrätz

July 26
Pre-peace negotiations held at Nikolsburg

August 18
North German Federation founded under Prussian leadership

August 22
Bavaria's representatives sign the peace treaty and a protection agreement with Prussia without the guarantees demanded by Ludwig II; in case of war the Bavarian army will be under Prussia's command;

Bavaria will pay reparations
and cede territories to Prussia
September 20
Prussia annexes Hanover,
Electorate of Hesse, Nassau,
and Frankfurt/Main; Austria
withdraws from German
Empire
November 10–December 10
Ludwig II travels to Franconia
December 25
Prince Otto decorates Bavarian
officers and soldiers of the
1866 war
December 31
Ludwig II appoints Prince
Chlodwig von Hohenlohe-
Schillingsfürst to replace von
der Pfordten as prime minister

1867 *January 22*
Ludwig engaged to Princess
Sophie, daughter of Duke
Maximilian of Bavaria and
sister of Empress Elisabeth of
Austria
May 31/June 1
Ludwig II and his brother
Otto travel to Eisenach and
visit the Wartburg
July 20–29
Ludwig II visits the Inter-
national World Fair in Paris
and talks with Napoleon III;
he declines an agreement be-
tween France and the southern
German states out of national
considerations; visits
Pierrefonds Castle
October 10
Engagement between
Ludwig II and Sophie of
Bavaria dissolved

1868 *February 29*
Ludwig I dies in southern
France
April 29
Ludwig II inaugurates Prince
Otto into the Order of the
Knights of St. George

June 21
Wagner's opera *The Mastersingers of Nuremberg* premiers
in the Court Theater in Munich
August 2–10
Ludwig II and his brother Otto
travel to Kissingen, meet with
the Russian czar and czarina
September 26
Czarina Maria Alexandrovna
visits Berg Castle

1869 *August 27*
Cornerstone for Schachen
Palace laid
September 5
Cornerstone for Neuschwan-
stein Castle laid
September 22
Richard Wagner's opera
Rhinegold premiers in the
Munich Court Theater
December 18
Queen Mother Marie calls for
the foundation of the Bavarian
Women's Society (later the
Bavarian Red Cross) with
Ludwig's support

1870 *January 17*
Opening of the state parlia-
ment attended by Prince Otto;
Ludwig II swears loyalty to
Prussia
March 7
Prime Minister Hohenlohe
forced to resign; Count Bray-
Steinburg appointed
June 26
Wagner's opera *Valkyrie*
premiers in Munich
July 14
Without consulting the king,
War Minister von Pranckh
pledges Bavarian support to
Prussia in case of a French
attack
July 15
The Council of Ministers
requests Ludwig II to order
mobilization

July 16
France declares war on Prussia;
Ludwig II orders general
mobilization against France;
Count Bray-Steinburg makes a
last attempt to negotiate peace
July 27
Gala performance at the Court
Theater in honor of the Prussian
crown prince; Prince Otto at-
tends Ludwig II's last Royal
Parade and departs to the
front to the headquarters of
the King of Prussia, later
Emperor William I
September 1
Battle of Sedan: French army
completely defeated with sup-
port of the 1st Bavarian Army;
Emperor Napoleon III cap-
tured by German troops and
imprisoned in Germany
September 13
Ludwig II announces to
Bismarck his willingness to
join a constitutional federation
September 30
Construction of Linderhof
Castle begins
October 20
Plenipotentiary delegates
Ministers Bray-Steinburg,
Lutz and Pranckh travel to
Versailles
November 23
Treaty of Versailles; Bavaria
enters the German Federation
and receives concessions
regarding federal prerogatives
November 30
Ludwig II writes the so-called
"Imperial Letter" to King
William I of Prussia urging
him to reinstitute the German
imperial crown and the Ger-
man Reich; letter delivered by
Prince Luitpold
1871 Prince Otto returns to Pruss-
ian headquarters; he is decor-

ated with the Iron Cross after
the campaign
January 18
Foundation of the German
Reich: King William I of
Prussia elected German emp-
eror; Prince Otto represents
his brother at the proclama-
tion; Bismarck becomes
Chancellor of the Reich
February 26
Pre-peace treaty of Versailles
between Germany and France:
Lorraine and Alsace become
part of the German Reich
April 16
Constitution of the German
Reich declared to takes effect
on May 4, 1871
May 10
Peace of Frankfurt/Main;
Prince Otto's mental disorder
worsens; he is committed to
medical care
July 16
Victorious Bavarian army
marches into Munich under
the leadership of Crown
Prince Frederick William of
Prussia; Ludwig II and the
Prussian Crown Prince meet
August 31–June 2, 1872
Count Friedrich von Hegnen-
berg-Dux succeeds Count
Bray-Steinburg as Bavarian
prime minister
November 15
Bismarck informed of Prince
Otto's mental disorder
1872 *March 19*
Ludwig purchases the theater
on Gärtner Square in Munich
May 5
Ludwig II views first "private
performance"
May 22
Cornerstone for the Festival
House in Bayreuth, built to
honor Richard Wagner, laid

1873 Prince Otto plans to move to
the Canary Islands
September 26
Herreninsel island in Lake
Chiemsee purchased by
Ludwig II

1874 *January*
Empress Elisabeth of Austria
visits a cholera hospital and
an insane asylum in Munich
August 20–28
Ludwig II goes to Paris
October 12
Queen Mother Marie converts
to the Catholic faith in
Waltenhofen

1875 *February 9*
Dr. Gudden provides medical
evaluation of Prince Otto's
mental state
May 27
Prince Otto's mental illness
breaks out; he is brought to
Schleissheim Castle, where he
stays until 1880
August 22
Ludwig II participates for the
last time in the Royal Parade
on the Marsfeld in Munich
August 24–27
Ludwig II travels to Rheims,
France, to trace the history of
Joan of Arc

1876 *August 6–9 and 27–31*
Ludwig II visits the Bayreuth
Festival to attend the premiere
of Wagner's *Ring*

1877 *August 25*
Venus Grotto at Linderhof
completed

1878 *May 11*
Assassination attempt on
German Emperor William I
May 21
Cornerstone for Herrenchiem-
see Castle laid
June 27
Ludwig II visits with Crown
Prince Rudolf of Austria, son

of Empress Elisabeth, on Rose
Island

1880 *March 13*
Prince Otto's illness worsens;
he is taken from Schleissheim
Palace to Fürstenried Castle
August 22
Ludwig II makes his last royal
proclamation to the Bavarian
people

1881 *March 13*
Czar Alexander II is assassin-
ated in a bomb attack; he is
succeeded by his son,
Alexander III
June 27–July 14
Ludwig II takes a trip to
Switzerland with actor Josef
Kainz

1882 *July 26*
Richard Wagner's opera
Parsifal premiers in the
Bayreuth Festival House

1883 *February 13*
Richard Wagner dies in
Venice

1884 *May 16*
Ludwig II purchases the ruins
of Falkenstein Castle
May 27–June 8
Ludwig II inhabits Neu-
schwanstein for the first and
only time

1885 *October 14*
Ludwig II and his mother
meet for the last time

1886 *June 8*
Doctors certify Ludwig II is
"mentally deranged"
June 9
Ludwig II declared
incompetent
June 10
Prince Luitpold assumes
regency; first commission
appears at Neuschwanstein
June 12
Second commission brings
Ludwig II to Berg Castle

June 13
Ludwig II dies, along with Dr. Gudden, in Lake Starnberg under unexplained circumstances

June 14
Official proclamation declares that the crown has passed to Prince Otto

1889 *May 17*
Queen Mother Marie dies at Hohenschwangau Castle

1912 *November 8*
Prince-Regent Luitpold, King Otto's deputy, dies at almost ninety years of age

December 12
Prince-Regent Luitpold's son Ludwig becomes King Ludwig III of Bavaria; Otto retains the title of king, but permanently loses all claim to actually reign, thus giving Bavaria two kings

1916 *October 11*
King Otto dies in Fürstenried Castle and is buried near his brother, Ludwig II, in the vault in St. Michael's Church in Munich

1918 In a coup, Kurt Eisner brings the Bavarian monarchy to an end and proclaims a republic

November 13
Ludwig III abdicates

1921 *October 21*
Ludwig III dies at Sárvár Castle in Hungary

Bibliography

Blunt, Wilfrid. The Dream King: Ludwig II of Bavaria. London, 1970.

Designs for the Dream King: the Castles and Palaces of King Ludwig II of Bavaria. London and New York, 1979.

Epp, Annette: Die Rosen singen Liebeslieder. Rosenheim 2004

Eyck, Erich. Bismarck and the German Empire. New York, 1964.

Gutman, Robert. Richard Wagner: The Man, his Mind, and his Music. Harcourt, 1990.

Haasen, Gisela: Ludwig II. – Briefe an seine Erzieherin. Munich 1995

Hamann, Brigitte. Sissi: Elisabeth, Empress of Austria. New York, 1997.

Haslip, Joan. The Lonely Empress: Elizabeth of Austria. London, 2000.

Knapp, Gottfried, et al. Neuschwanstein. Munich, 2000.

Krückmann, Peter Oluf, translated by Rosie Jackson. The King and his Castle: Neuschwanstein. Munich and New York, 2001.

McIntosh, Christoher. Ludwig II of Bavaria, the Swan King. London and New York, 1997.

Merten, Klaus, editor, et. al. German Castles and Palaces. New York, 1999.

Sailer, Anton, translated by Sheila Ickerott. Castles, Mystery and Music: The Legend of Ludwig II, a Pictorial History of the Life of Ludwig II of Bavaria. Munich, 1983.

Schad, Martha. Die Familiengeschichte der Wittelsbacher in Bildern. Regensburg, 1994/ Augsburg, 1999.

Schad, Martha. Kaiserin Elisabeth und ihre Töchter. Munich, 1997.

Schad, Martha. Elisabeth von Österreich. Munich, 2003 (4th edition).

Schad, Martha. Bayerns Königinnen. Regensburg, 2004 (4th edition).

Schad, Martha: Romanzen auf der Roseninsel. Rosenheim 2004

Schad, Martha: Marie Valerie – Das Tagebuch der Lieblingstochter der Kaiserin Elisabeth. Munich 2005 (12th edition)

Schad, Martha and Horst. Cosima Wagner und Ludwig II. von Bayern—Briefe: Eine erstaunliche Korrespondenz. Bergisch Gladbach, 1996.

Skelton, Geoffrey, editor; translated by Martin Gregor-Dellin. Cosima Wagner's Diaries: An Abridgement. New Haven, 1997.

Spancer, Stewart. Wagner Remembered. New York, 2000.

Spotts, Frederic. Bayreuth: A History of the Wagner Festival. New Haven, 1994.

Von Burg, Katerina. Ludwig II of Bavaria: The Man and the Mystery. London, 1989.

Waller, Bruce. Bismarck (Historical Association Studies). New York, 1997.

Wetzel, David. A Duel of Giants: Bismarck, Napoleon III and the Origins of the Franco-Prussian War. Madison, Wisconsin, 2001.

Index

Picture Credits